BANKRUPTCY: A PRIMER

BANKRUPTCY: A PRIMER

D. ELLSWORTH BLANC

Novinka Books
New York

#50012320

Senior Editors: Susan Boriotti and Donna Dennis
Coordinating Editor: Tatiana Shohov
Office Manager: Annette Hellinger
Graphics: Wanda Serrano
Book Production: Matthew Kozlowski, Jonathan Rose and Jennifer Vogt
Circulation: Raymond Davis, Cathy DeGregory, Ave Maria Gonzalez
and Jonathan Roque
Communications and Acquisitions: Serge P. Shohov

Library of Congress Cataloging-in-Publication Data
Available Upon Request

ISBN 1-59033-218-0.

Copyright © 2002 by Novinka Books
An Imprint of Nova Science Publishers, Inc.
227 Main Street, Suite 100
Huntington, New York 11743
Tele. 631-424-NOVA (6682)   Fax 631-425-5933
E Mail: Novascience@earthlink.net
www.novapublishers.com

CONTENTS

PREFACE

For many businesses, bankruptcy is a looming reality, one that can take many forms. Bankruptcy is such a fact of life that a tangle of laws exist in the U.S. legal code. The most widely recognized type, Chapter 11, permits the reorganization, as opposed to the liquidation, of financially troubled businesses. An economic analysis has to start with the observation that business failure is not always bad, as efficiency in the economy demands continual reallocation of resources. This book offers a thorough overview of the bankruptcy laws and procedures American businesses and consumers are faced with.

A BANKRUPTCY PRIMER: LIQUIDATION AND REORGANIZATION UNDER THE U.S. BANKRUPTCY CODE

Robin Jeweler

This report examines the legal procedures for effecting either a liquidation or a business or consumer reorganization under one of three of the five operative chapters of the United State Bankruptcy Code, 11 U.S. C. § 101 *et seq.*[1] Chapter 7 of the Code governs liquidation of the debtor's estate and is often referred to as a "straight bankruptcy." Chapter 11 of the Code governs business reorganizations, and chapter 13 governs consumer reorganizations which conform to prescribed statutory debt limits.

---

[1] Chapters 1, 3, and 5 of the Bankruptcy Code establish general procedures which are applicable to each of the operative chapters, i.e., chapters 7, 9, 11, 12, and 13.

Chapter 9, which deals with adjustments of debts of a municipality, and chapter 12, which deals with family farmer reorganization, are not addressed in this report. Also omitted are subchapters dealing with stockbroker liquidation, 11 U.S. C. §§ 741 – 752; commodity broker liquidation, 11 U.S. C. §§ 761 – 766; and railroad reorganization, 11 U.S. C. §§ 1161 – 1171.

INTRODUCTION: CAPSULE HISTORY
OF THE U.S. BANKRUPTCY LAWS

The United States Constitution expressly delegates to the Congress the power "To establish...uniform Laws on the subject of Bankruptcies throughout the United States."[2] It was not until 1800, however, that the United States enacted its first bankruptcy law,[3] and that act was repealed shortly thereafter in 1803.[4] Enactment of the law was motivated by severe financial panics in the 1790's that resulted in the imprisonment of many debtors.[5] A second act was approved August 19, 1841[6] and repealed in 1843.[7] Like its predecessor, the Act of 1841 arose from a period of economic hardship and was short-lived. A subsequent law, the Act of 1867,[8] followed the financial disturbances incident to the Civil War. In effect for more than a decade, it was repealed in 1878.[9] Thus, throughout a period of some 78 years, a national bankruptcy law was operative for only 16. After the repeal of the Act of 1867, a period of some 20 years would pass before another bankruptcy act was forthcoming – the Act of 1898.[10]

The Act of 1898 followed a depression of several years duration beginning in 1893. Among the reasons cited by Congress in support of a new and permanent bankruptcy law was the increasing availability to the public of an expanding network of federal courts, and increasing national growth of both population and commerce.[11] The 1898 Act was amended at various times but underwent a comprehensive revision and modernization in 1938.[12] These amendments, effected by a law known as the Chandler Act, recast the relief provisions that had been added to the 1898 Act, established wage earner plans, and substituted or replaced provisions dealing with real

---

[2] Article I, section 8, clause 4.
[3] 2 Stat. 19 (April 4, 1800).
[4] 2 Stat. 248 (December 9, 1803).
[5] 1 Norton Bankr. L. & Prac.   1.02.
[6] 5 Stat. 440 (August 19, 1841).
[7] 5 Stat 614 (March 3, 1843).
[8] 14 Stat. 517 (March 2, 1867).
[9] 20 Stat. 99 (June 7, 1878).
[10] 30 Stat. 544 (July 1, 1898).
[11] H.Rept. 1228, 54th Congress, 1st Session Incorporated in H.Rept. 65, 55th Congress, 2d Session 29-30 (1897).
[12] 52 Stat. 840 (June 22, 1938).

property arrangements and corporate reorganizations. Changes in the Act subsequent to the 1938 amendments were relatively slight.[13]

Eventually, Congress perceived a need to modernize the bankruptcy laws, and, in 1970, it created a Commission on the Bankruptcy Laws of the United States to study and recommend changes in the law.[14] The Commission became operational in June, 1971, and filed its final report with the Congress on July 30, 1973.[15]

Among the reasons expressed by Congress for enactment of a new and modernized Bankruptcy Code was that the substantive law of bankruptcy embodied in the Act of 1898 reflected "the horse and buggy" era of consumer and commercial credit; that the widespread adoption of the Uniform Commercial Code in the early 1970's changed and expanded commercial financing; that bankruptcy relief for the consumer debtor was inadequate; and, that the bankruptcy court system was too frequently an inefficient and unfair forum.[16]

Hence, the stage was set for a national debate on the bankruptcy laws. In 1978, Congress repealed the Act of 1898 in its entirety and enacted the present Bankruptcy Code, the Bankruptcy Reform Act of 1978.[17]

Since the Code's enactment in 1978, it has undergone several major amendments. The Bankruptcy Amendments and Federal Judgeship Act of 1984[18] cured constitutional deficiencies in the bankruptcy court system[19] and made a wide variety of substantive and technical amendments to the Code. The Bankruptcy Judges, United States Trustees, and Family Farmer Bankruptcy Act of 1986 instituted a nation-wide U.S. Trustee system and added a new operative chapter governing reorganizations of "family farmers."[20] In 1988, Congress enacted several substantive amendments to the Code, including the Retiree Benefits Bankruptcy Protection Act, which

---

[13] Among post-1938 amendments were major revisions to the provisions governing municipal reorganization under chapter 9 which were enacted in response to New York City's financial crisis. See, P.L. 94-260, 90 Stat. 315 (1976).

[14] P.L. 91-354, 84 Stat. 468 (July 24, 1970).

[15] Report of the Commission on Bankruptcy Laws, H.R. Doc. No. 137, parts I and II, 93rd Congress, 1st Session (1973).

[16] H.Rept. 95-595, 95th Congress, 1st Session 4-5 (1977) (Report of the House Committee on the Judiciary to accompany H.R. 8200.) See also, S.Rept. 95-989, 95th Congress, 2d Session (1978) (Report of the Senate Committee on the Judiciary to accompany S. 2266.) These reports comprise, in part, the legislative history of the Bankruptcy Reform Act.

[17] P.L. 95-598, 92 Stat. 2549 (November 6, 1978).

[18] P.L. 98-353, 98 Stat. 333 (July 10, 1984).

[19] See Northern Pipeline Construction Co. V. Marathon Pipe Line Co., 458 U.S. 50 (1982).

[20] P.L. 99-554, 100 Stat. 3088 (October 27, 1986). Originally designated to sunset on October 1, 1993, chapter 12 was extended through October 1, 1998 by P.L. 103-65, 107 Stat. 311 (Aug. 6, 1993).

added a new section governing the rights of retirees of a corporation undergoing a chapter 11 reorganization.[21]

During the 101st Congress, more amendments were enacted. In addition to technical amendments affecting swap agreements and forward contracts,[22] legislation was passed altering the dischargeability under chapters 7 and 13, respectively, for debts for liability incurred while driving while intoxicated, criminal restitution, and student loans.[23] The Comprehensive Thrift and Bank Fraud Prosecution and Taxpayer Recovery Act of 1990[24] made many amendments designed to strengthen criminal prosecution of and recovery from crimes against banks.

The most recent congressional enactment making wide-reaching substantive and procedural amendments to the Code took place pursuant to the Bankruptcy Reform Act of 1994.[25] Among its highlights was the creation of a National Bankruptcy Review Commission, patterned after the 1970 Commission, to study and report within two years recommendations for legislative or administrative action to the President, the Congress, and the Supreme Court. The Commission issued its report on October 20, 1997.[26] In a lengthy report of approximately 1300 pages, the Commission adopted as many as 172 recommendations dealing with *inter alia*, consumer bankruptcy, business bankruptcy, municipal bankruptcy, and, bankruptcy jurisdiction, procedure, and administration. On the subject of consumer bankruptcy reform, the Commission could not reach consensus. Recommendations were adopted by a 5-4 split vote, which undermined the persuasive value and influence on the Congress of the Commission's report.[27]

Important procedural reform effected by the 1994 Act included express authorization for bankruptcy courts to conduct jury trials *with* the consent of parties thereto. The Act also encouraged nation-wide creation of Bankruptcy

---

[21] P.L. 100-334, 102 Stat. 610 (June 16, 1988), codified at 11 U.S. C. § 1114. See also, P.L. 100-506, 102 Stat. 2538 (Oct. 18, 1988) (involving executory contract licensing rights to intellectual property), and P.L. 100-597, 102 Stat. 3028 (Nov. 3, 1988) (amending chapter 9 provisions governing municipal reorganization).

[22] P.L. 101-311, 104 Stat. 267 (June 25, 1990).

[23] P.L. 101-508 (Nov. 5, 1990), the Omnibus Budget Reconciliation Act; P.L. 101-581 (Nov. 15, 1990), the Criminal Victims Protection Act of 1990; P.L. 101-647 (Nov. 29, 1990), the Crime Control Act of 1990.

[24] Title XXVII of P.L. 101-647.

[25] P.L. 103-394, 108 Stat. 4106 (October 22, 1994).

[26] "Bankruptcy: The Next Twenty Years," National Bankruptcy Review Commission Final Report (GPO, October 20, 1997). The report is accessible on the Internet: <http://www.access.gpo.gov/nbrc>.

[27] See, "Recommendations for Reform of Consumer Bankruptcy Law by Four Dissenting Commissioners," id.

Appellate Panels as intermediary, specialized review tribunals positioned between U.S. district court and the circuit courts of appeals. This law also incorporated sanctions into the Code for negligent or fraudulent bankruptcy petition preparers and amends federal criminal law to establish additional penalties for bankruptcy fraud.

The 105th Congress considered, but did not enact, major bankruptcy reform legislation.[28] Several provisions were enacted, however, including the Religious Liberty and Charitable Donation Protection Act,[29] permitting debtors to make substantial charitable donations prior to filing and during the course of a chapter 13 reorganization. Other provisions narrowed the dischargeability of student loans, and effected amendments to the automatic stay.

STRUCTURE OF THE U.S. BANKRUPTCY CODE

The Code is divided into eight chapters – chapters 1, 3, 5, 7, 9 11, 12, and 13. Chapters 1, 3, and 5 govern general procedures involving management and administration of the bankruptcy estate which are applicable, as specified, to the operative chapters. Chapters 7 through 13, the operative chapters, address the different forms of bankruptcy relief, i.e., liquidation or the various categories of reorganization – municipal, business, family farmer, and consumer.

Also codified under Title 11 of the United States Code are Rules of Bankruptcy Court and officially authorized bankruptcy forms.

Examined below are substantive highlights of the procedural and operative provisions of the U.S. Bankruptcy Code governing liquidation and reorganization.

---

[28] See, H.Rept. 104-794, 105th Congress, 2d Sess. (1998), Conference Report to accompany H.R. 3150, the Bankruptcy Reform Act of 1998.

[29] P.L. 105-183, 112 Stat. 517 (June 19, 1998).

OVERVIEW OF THE U.S. BANKRUPTCY CODE PROVISIONS GOVERNING LIQUIDATION AND REORGANIZATION
I. CASE ADMINISTRATION

A. Who May Be a Debtor?

Any debtor that is a person, partnership or corporation residing, domiciled, having property or a place of business in the United States may file for relief under the Bankruptcy Code, except that:

1. Several entities may not file for liquidation under chapter 7, namely, a railroad, an insurance company, bank, savings bank, cooperative bank, savings and loan association, homestead association, small business investment company, credit union, or federally guaranteed industrial bank.
2. A chapter 11 reorganization may only be filed by debtors that may file under chapter 7 (with the exception of railroads, stockbrokers, and commodity brokers who may also file under chapter 11.)
3. A chapter 13 reorganization is limited to an individual (and spouse) with regular income (except stockbrokers and commodity brokers) whose aggregate unsecured and secured debts are less than $269,250 and $807,750 respectively.
4. No individual or family farmer may file who has been a debtor in a case pending in the preceding 180 days if the case was dismissed for willful failure of the debtor to abide by orders of the court, or to appear before the court in proper prosecution of the case, or if the debtor obtained a voluntary dismissal following the filing of a request for relief from the automatic stay. 11 U.S.C. § 109.

B. Commencement of a Case

1. Voluntary Cases

A voluntary case is commenced when the debtor files a petition under the operative chapter of the Code in which the debtor desires to proceed. A husband and wife may file jointly, in which case the court will determine the extent, if any, to which the debtor's estate shall be consolidated.

Commencement of a voluntary case constitutes an order for relief. 11 U.S.C. §§ 301, 302.

2. Involuntary Cases

An involuntary, that is, a creditor-initiated bankruptcy may be commenced under chapter 7 or 11 of the Code. Among the creditor groups entitled to file is a group comprised of three or more creditors who hold at least $10,000 in noncontingent, nondisputed claims. Farmers, family farmers, and non-moneyed, noncommercial corporations may not be forced into bankruptcy involuntarily.

Although creditors may file a petition under the Code, it does not operate as an order for relief. The debtor may controvert the petition at trial, and until the court finds for the creditors and enters an order for relief, the debtor may operate its business as if a petition had not been filed. The court may, however, appoint either an interim trustee or a U.S. Trustee to manage the estate of the debtor pending an order for relief if the court believes it is necessary to preserve the estate.

The court may enter an order for relief against a debtor if, at trial, it finds that the debtor is generally not paying debts as they become due, or, if, within 120 days before the filing of the petition, a custodian was appointed or took possession of substantially all of the debtor's property.

If the court dismisses an involuntary petition against a debtor after trial other than on consent of all petitioners and the debtor, it may award the debtor costs, a reasonable attorney's fee, and, if any of the petitioners filed in bad faith, damages or punitive damages. 11 U.S.C. § 303.

C. Abstention

The bankruptcy court may dismiss a case or suspend all proceedings if, among other reasons, it finds that to do so would be in the best interests of creditors and that the debtor would be better served thereby.[30] An order dismissing or suspending an action is nonreviewable by appeal or otherwise. 11 U.S.C. § 305.

---

[30] An example of a situation where a court may find that a suspension or dismissal is warranted might arise when an arrangement is being worked out by the creditors and the debtor out of court, but an involuntary case has been commenced by a few recalcitrant creditors to provide a basis for future threats to extract full payment. The less expensive out-of-court workout may better serve the interests of the case. S.Rept. 95-989, supra note 16 at 36.

D. Debtor's Transactions with Attorneys

Attorneys representing debtors are required to file a statement of their compensation agreement with the court. If the court finds that the agreed to compensation exceeds the reasonable value of the services to be provided by the attorney, the court may cancel the agreement or order the return of the excess compensation paid to either the estate, or to the entity that made the payment if the property would not have come into the estate. 11 U.S.C. § 329.

E. Meeting of Creditors and Equity Security Holders

Within a reasonable time after an order for relief is entered, the United States Trustee must convene and preside at a meeting of creditors. The Trustee may order a meeting of any equity security holders. The bankruptcy court may *not* preside over or attend these creditor meetings.

In a chapter 7 case, the trustee must orally examine the debtor to ensure that the or she is aware of: the potential consequences of seeking a discharge in bankruptcy, including the effects on credit history; the debtor's ability to file under a different chapter; the effect of receiving a discharge; and, the effect of reaffirming a debt that would otherwise be dischargeable in bankruptcy. 11 U.S.C. § 341.

F. Examination of the Debtor and Self-Incrimination

The debtor must be available for examination under oath at the creditor's meeting. "Use" immunity may be granted to all persons required to testify, be examined, or provide information in a bankruptcy case. 11 U.S.C. §§ 343, 344.

G. Conversion from One Chapter to Another

1. Effect of Conversion

After notice, a case may be converted from one chapter to another. Conversion does not change the date of the original filing of the petition, the commencement of the case, or the order for review, but it does terminate the services of the trustee serving in the case prior to conversion. Claims against the debtor that arise after the petition but before the conversion shall be treated as prepetition claims. 11 U.S.C. § 348.

2. Conversion from Chapter 7

A debtor may convert a case from chapter 7 to one under chapters 11, 12, or 13, if the case has not already been converted from one of those chapters. A party in interest may request a conversion of the debtor's case from chapter 7 to chapter 11, but not to chapter 12 or 13. 11 U.S.C. § 706.

3. Conversion from Chapter 11

A debtor may convert a case from chapter 11 to one under chapter 7 unless (1) the debtor is not in possession of the estate, (2) the case was filed as an involuntary case under chapter 11, or (3) the case was already converted to one under chapter 11 upon another party's request.

The court itself may convert the case from a chapter 11 reorganization to a chapter 7 liquidation "for cause," which includes continuing loss or diminution of the estate and absence of a reasonable likelihood of rehabilitation; inability to effectuate a plan; unreasonable delay by the debtor that is prejudicial to creditors; or, failure to meet the statutory requirements to effect and implement a reorganization plan. The court may not convert a case to chapter 7 if the debtor is a farmer, and may convert a case to chapter 12 or 13 only if the debtor requests the conversion.

A case may also be converted to one under chapter 7 on request of the U.S. Trustee when a debtor fails to file its list of creditors, schedule or assets and liabilities, and other required information in conformance with statutory requirements. 11 U.S.C. § 1112.

4. Conversion from Chapter 13

A debtor under chapter 13 may convert a case to one under chapter 7 at any time. Property of the estate in the converted case shall consist of property as of the date of the initial filing. If the conversion occurs in "bad faith," property of the estate may be valued as of the date of conversion, thereby encompassing after-acquired property. 11 U.S.C. § 348(f).

A party in interest in chapter 13 may request that the court convert the case to one under chapter 7 "for cause," but may request conversion to either chapter 11 or 12 at any time before confirmation of a plan. The Court may not convert a chapter 13 case to another chapter if the debtor is otherwise ineligible to be a debtor thereunder, or if the debtor is a farmer, unless the debtor requests such conversion. 11 U.S.C. § 1307.

H. Dismissal

1. Effect of Dismissal

Unless otherwise ordered by the court, dismissal of a case does not bar discharge in a later case of debts that were dischargeable in the dismissed case.

Dismissal does reinstate prior, superseded custodianships and proceedings, voided transfers and liens, and revests estate property in the entity in which the property was vested immediately prior to the commencement of the case. 11 U.S.C. § 349.

2. Dismissal of a Chapter 7 Case

The court may dismiss a case only "for cause," including unreasonable delay by the debtor that is prejudicial to creditors; nonpayment of fees; or, failure by the debtor to file a list of creditors, a schedule of assets and liabilities, and other necessary information.

The court, on its own motion, or on the motion of a U.S. Trustee, may dismiss a case filed by an individual debtor whose debts are primarily consumer debts if it finds that granting relief would be a substantial abuse of the provisions of chapter 7. There is a presumption in favor of granting the requested relief. 11 U.S.C. § 707.

3. Dismissal of a Chapter 11 Case

As in the case of conversions requested by a party other than a debtor, the court may dismiss a case only after notice and hearing "for cause." 11 U.S.C. § 1112.

4. Dismissal of a Chapter 13 Case

The court may dismiss a case only "for cause," including:

- unreasonable delay or gross mismanagement by the debtor that is prejudicial to creditors;
- nonpayment of necessary fees and charges;

- failure to file a plan;
- failure to begin payments required by a plan;
- denial of confirmation of a plan;
- material default b the debtor under a confirmed plan; or
- continuing loss to or diminution of the estate and absence of a reasonable likelihood of rehabilitation.

Additional ground for dismissal in a chapter 13 case include the debtor's failure to file required information concerning consumer debt. 11 U.S.C. ' 1307.

I. Bankruptcy Fees

Parties commencing a bankruptcy case must pay the clerk of the bankruptcy court the prescribed filing fees. Currently, filing fees are $130 for a case under chapter 7 or 13, and $800 for a case under chapter 11 that does not concern a railroad. An individual filing a voluntary case or a joint case may pay the fee in installments. For converting, on request of the debtor, a case from chapter 7 or 13 to one under chapter 11, the debtor must pay a fee of $400.

An individual filing under chapter 11 may pay the filing fee in installments. In addition to a filing fee, chapter 11 debtors pay a quarterly fee to the U.S. Trustee for each quarter until a plan is closed or the case is converted to dismissed. The fee is derived from a sliding scale based upon the amount of disbursements per quarter. 28 U.S.C. § 1930.

In chapter 13 cases, a standing trustee is permitted to charge a percentage fee, established by the U.S. Attorney General, not to exceed ten percent, from all payments received by the trustee for disbursement under the reorganization plan. 28 U.S.C. § 586.

II. UNITED STATES TRUSTEES AND OFFICERS OF THE BANKRUPTCY ESTATE

A. Background on the U.S. Trustee Program

When the Bankruptcy Reform Act was enacted in 1978, one of its basic goals was to remove bankruptcy judges from case administration.[31] Congress found bankruptcy judges to be too mired in the administrative details of bankruptcy cases and the creation of the office of the U.S. Trustee was designed to permit bankruptcy judges to handle only judicial matters.[32]

Under the 1978 Act, the U.S. Trustee program was implemented on an experimental basis with 10 "pilot" districts, one in each federal judicial circuit. The Bankruptcy Judges, United States Trustees, and Family Farmer Bankruptcy Act of 1986 established the U.S. Trustee system permanently and nation-wide.[33]

United States Trustees are appointed by, are subject to removal by, and remain under the direction of the United States Attorney General through the Executive Office for United States Trustees in the Department of Justice.

The U.S. Trustee system is funded through bankruptcy filing fees and "user" fees, that is, percentage fees charged by a trustee administering either a chapter 12 or 13 reorganization plan which are remitted to the United States Trustee System Fund. 28 U.S.C. §§ 586, 589a.

B. Duties of the U.S. Trustee

Although U.S. Trustees may serve directly as trustees in a chapter 7, 11, 12, or 13 bankruptcy, their duties are administrative.[34] They establish and supervise panels of private trustees that are eligible to serve in chapter 7 liquidations, and supervise the administration of cases and trustees under chapters 7, 11, 12 and 13. U.S. Trustees may, when necessary, appoint one

---

[31] 124 Cong. Rec. H11088, 11116 (daily ed. Sept. 28, 1978); 124 Cong. Rec. S17432 (daily ed. Oct. 6, 1978).

[32] H.Rept. 95-595, supra note 16 at 88-91.

[33] Note 20, supra.

[34] A detailed examination of the U.S. Trustee program, including the U.S. Trustee's administrative responsibilities under Title 28 of the U.S. Code, is beyond the scope of this report. Emphasis herein is on the respective roles of a U.S. Trustee, a private trustee, or a standing trustee in a liquidation or reorganization under the Code.

or more individuals to serve as standing trustees in chapter 12 or 13 cases. 28 U.S.C. §§ 581, 586.

Pursuant to amendments of the Bankruptcy Reform Act of 1994,[35] the U.S. Trustee is directed to review professional fee applications under procedural guidelines adopted by the Executive Office of the U.S. Trustee. 11 U.S.C. § 321.

C. Role of the U.S. Trustee under the Code

In addition to those responsibilities specifically delegated to the U.S. Trustee under the operative chapters of the Code, the U.S. Trustee is permitted to raise and appear and be heard on any issue in any case under the Code. 11 U.S.C. § 307.

D. Appointment of a Trustee Other Than a U.S. Trustee

A trustee is always appointed to oversee a chapter 7 liquidation and a reorganization under chapter 13. A trustee is appointed in a chapter 11 reorganization only "for cause" or when the court finds that to do so would be in the best interest of creditors. 11 U.S.C. §§, 1104, 1302.

E. Qualifications and Eligibility under the Code to Serve as a Trustee

In addition to those qualifications which may be established by the Attorney General to guide the U.S. Trustee in selecting panels of private trustees, the Code itself contains certain eligibility criteria. An individual must reside in the judicial district or adjacent to the district in which the cases is pending, and may not have served as an examiner in the case. A person selected to serve as trustee must file with the court a bond (the amount of which is determined by the U.S. Trustee) in favor of the United States conditioned on the faithful performance of official duties. 11 U.S. C. §§ 321, 322.

---

[35] Note 25, supra at § 224(a).

F. Removal of a Trustee

The court may, after notice and hearing, remove a trustee, other than a U.S. Trustee, for cause. 11 U.S. C. § 324.

G. Employment and Compensation of Professionals by a Trustee

The trustee is permitted, with the court's approval, to employ attorneys, accountants, appraisers, or other professionals to assist in the administration of the bankruptcy case. When a trustee operates a debtor's business, and the debtor had regularly employed such professionals, the trustee may retain or replace them. The court may authorize the trustee to serve as attorney or accountant to the estate if it would be in the best interests of the estate.

The court oversees compensation of professionals retained by a trustee. 11 U.S.C. §§ 327, 328.

The court may award reasonable compensation for services rendered by a trustee of professional or paraprofessional and reimbursement for actual, necessary expenses.

The court may, on its own motion or on motion of the U.S. Trustee, or any party in interest, award compensation that is less than the amount requested.

Factors to be considered by the court measure the nature, extent, and value of the services, including the time spent rendering the service and the rate charged; whether the services were necessary or beneficial towards completion of the estate; whether the services were performed within a reasonable amount of time commensurate with the complexity, importance and nature of the problem; and, whether the compensation is reasonable based on the customary rates charged by comparably skilled practitioners in cases other than bankruptcy.[36] 11 U.S. C. § 330.

H. Compensation of Trustees

The Code imposes limits upon private trustee compensation in chapters 7 and 11. A trustee may not realize more than 25% on the first $5,000 or

---

[36] Express standards for court review of fee awards was effected by § 224 of the 1994 Bankruptcy Reform Act, supra note 25.

less, 10% on any amount in excess of $5,000 but less than $50,000, 5% on any amount in excess of $50,000 but less than $1,000,000, and compensation not to exceed 3% of money in excess of $1,000,000 disbursed by the bankruptcy estate. 11 U.S.C. § 326.

A chapter 7 trustee also receives $45 to be paid from the filing fee, which may be increased by an additional $15 from fees prescribed by the Judicial Conference of the United States. 11 U.S.C. § 330(b).[37]

III. ADMINISTRATIVE POWERS

A. The Automatic Stay

The automatic stay is triggered when an order for relief is filed. The stay is generally acknowledged to be one of the fundamental debtor protections provided by the bankruptcy laws. It gives the debtor a "breathing spell" from his creditors because it stops all collection efforts, all harassment, and all foreclosure actions. It permits the debtor to attempt a repayment or reorganization plan, or simply to be relieved of the financial pressures that drove him into bankruptcy.[38]

By halting all collection activities, the stay provides creditor protection as well. Without it, certain creditors would be able to pursue their own remedies against the debtor's property. The stay prevents the piecemeal dismantling of the debtor's property in ways that would be preferential to some creditors and detrimental to others.

The bankruptcy petition, which in a voluntary case is the order for relief, operates to stay:

- all prepetition process or proceedings of an administrative or judicial nature, or to recover a claim, that were or could have been brought before commencement of the case;
- enforcement of prepetition judgments against the debtor or his property;
- acts to obtain possession of estate property;
- acts to create, perfect or enforce property liens securing prepetition claims;

---

[37] Id. at § 117.
[38] H.Rept. 95-595, supra note 16 at 340.

- acts to create, perfect, maintain, or continue perfection, or enforce any lien against estate property;
- acts to collect, assess or recover on prepetition claims;
- the set-off of prepetition debts owed to debtor against any claim against the debtor;[39]
- United States Tax Court proceedings.

But, there are exceptions to actions stayed by the order for relief. They include:

- criminal proceedings;
- actions to establish paternity; to establish or modify an order for alimony, maintenance or support; or, to collect alimony, maintenance or support from nonestate property;[40]
- actions to enforce a governmental unit's police or regulatory power, or a judgment (other than a money judgment) obtained by such power;[41]
- the set-off of any mutual debt and claim for specified transactions involving commodity brokers, forward contracts merchants, stockbrokers, securities clearing agencies, repo participants, or swap agreement participants;

---

[39] A creditor bank did not violate the automatic stay by protecting its right to setoff by temporarily withholding payment of a debt to the debtor as it sought relief from the automatic stay. The debtor had defaulted on loan payments to the bank, which placed a postpetition "administrative hold" on the debtor's bank account. Citizens Bank of Maryland v. Strumpf, 116 S. Ct. 286 (1995).

[40] The automatic stay is inapplicable to actions to collect alimony or child support from nonestate property. In chapter 7, nonestate property is property acquired by the debtor postpetition. But, in chapter 13, a debtor pledges disposable postpetition property to the reorganization plan. Prior to the child support and alimony amendments in § 304 of the Bankruptcy Reform Act of 1994, the Code was silent on the status of these payments in the bankruptcy scheme. Even though they were nondischargeable, are priority payments in bankruptcy. Subsection 304(g) of the Act also confers upon child support creditors or their representatives permission to appear and intervene in bankruptcy court proceedings "without meeting any special local court rule requirement for attorney appearances" upon filing of a form that contains information detailing the debt, its status and other characteristics.

[41] This exception was amended in 1998 to include certain actions by "any organization exercising authority under the Convention on the Prohibition of the Development, Production, Stockpiling and use of Chemical Weapons and on Their Destruction" to enforce the organization's police or regulatory power derived from the chemical weapons treaty. P.L. 105-277, § 603 (October 21, 1998).

- actions by the Secretary of Housing and Urban Development to foreclose or take possession in a case of a loan insured under the National Housing Act;
- an audit by a governmental unit to determine tax liability; the issuance of tax deficiency notice; a demand for tax returns; or, the making of an assessment and issuance of a note for demand and payment (although tax liens that might otherwise attach to estate property will be stayed unless such tax is nondischargeable and such property or its proceeds are transferred out of the estate and revested in the debtor);[42]
- actions by a lessor to the debtor under a lease of nonresidential real property that has terminated before or during the case to obtain possession of such property.
- presentation, notice, and protest of the dishonoring of a negotiable instrument;
- actions by a state licensing agency regarding the accreditation status of licensure of a debtor education institution, or by a guaranty agency or the Secretary of Education regarding the eligibility of the debtor to participate in authorized programs; or
- the creation or perfection of a statutory lien for an ad valorem property tax imposed by the District of Columbia, or a political subdivision of a state, if such tax comes due after the filing of the petition.

                                        11 U.S.C. § 362 (a) & (b).

B. Relief from Automatic Stays

1. Judicial Relief

A creditor, or other party in interest, may request the court to terminate, modify, annul, or condition a stay with respect to a specific asset of the debtor. The court, after notice and hearing, may grant relief:

a. for cause, including the lack of adequate protection of the interested party's interest in such property; or
b. with respect to a stay of an act against property, if –
(i)   the debtor has no equity in such property;

---

[42] This exception to the stay was expanded from the issuance of a notice of tax deficiency by § 116 of the 1994 Reform Act, supra note 25.

(ii)   such property is not necessary to a reorganization; or

(iii)   a "single asset" debtor, has not, within 90 days of the order for relief, filed a feasible plan for reorganization, or has commenced monthly payments to secured creditors which represent an amount equal to interest at a current fair market rate on the value of the creditor's interest in the real estate.[43]

If the court does not rule within 90 days from a request by motion for relief from the stay, the stay is automatically terminated with respect to the property in question. The court may, however, grant relief without a hearing when necessary to prevent irreparable damage to the interest of an entity in property if the damage will occur before there is an opportunity for notice and hearing. 11 U.S.C. § 362(d),(e)&(f).

2. Removal of Property From the Estate; Termination of the Case

A stay may terminate by reason of provisions relating to its duration, for example, the property is no longer property of the estate. The stay of any other act continues until the case is closed, dismissed, or a discharge is granted or denied. 11 U.S.C. § 362(c).

C. Adequate Protection

The concept of "adequate protection" of a secured creditor's interest in property is derived from the fifth amendment protection of property interests as enunciated by the U.S. Supreme Court.[44] When an automatic stay, or the sale, use or lease of estate property by the trustee or debtor in possession results in a decrease in value of the legal or equitable interests of the secured creditor or co-owner with the debtor of such property, such decrease in value may be adequately protected by:

---

[43] Provisions regarding "single asset" debtors were added to the Code by virtue of § 218 of the 1994 Reform Act. "Single asset real estate" means a single property which generates substantially all of the gross income of a debtor; a property on which no substantial business is being conducted by a debtor other than the operation thereof; and, a property having aggregate noncontingent, liquidated secured debts in an amount less than $4,000,000. 11 U.S.C. § 101(51B).

[44] See United States v. Security Industrial Bank, 459 U.S. 70 (1982); Wright v. Union Central Life Ins. Co., 311 U.S. 273, rehearing denied 312 U.S. 711 (1940); Louisville Joint Stock Land Bank v. Radford, 295 U.S. 555 (1935). See also, Sen. Rep. 95-989, supra note 16 at 49.

- periodic cash payments to the extent of such decrease; of
- providing additional or replacement liens to the extent of such decrease; or
- granting other relief which results in the realization by the secured creditor of the "indubitable equivalent" of such entity's interest in the property.[45]

11 U.S.C. § 361.

D. Use, Sale or Lease of Property

The Code sets out in detail the rights of a trustee or debtor in possession to use, sell, or lease property of the estate in the operation of the debtor's business in either a liquidation or reorganization. The thrust of this section is the protection of secured creditors and other parties who have interests in the property involved, and they are framed primarily as limitations or conditions upon the debtor's right to use, sell, or lease estate property.

Estate property may be used, sold, or leased by the trustee:

- other than in the ordinary course of business only after notice and hearing;
- in the ordinary course of business, without notice and hearing if the operation of the debtor's business is authorized and the court has not ordered otherwise;
- on consent of all parties having an interest, or on court authority after notice and hearing, if the property involved is defined as cash collateral, namely, cash, negotiable instruments, documents of title, securities, deposit accounts, or other cash equivalents;
- if it is not inconsistent with any relief from an automatic or other stay granted to a party having an interest in estate property;
- if adequate protection of an entity's interest in the property has been provided.

11 U.S.C. § 362 (a)-(e).

---

[45] The "indubitable equivalent" criterion does not entitle an undersecured creditor to compensation for the delay caused by the automatic stay in foreclosing on the collateral, often referred to as "lost opportunity costs." United Saving Assoc. of Texas v. Timbers of Inwood Forest Assoc., 484 U.S. 365 (1988).

Subject to specified conditions, the trustee may sell property free and clear of the interests of spouses and co-owners so long as they receive either a right of first refusal at the price at which the sale is being consummated, or an appropriate portion of the sale proceeds. 11 U.S.C. § 363(h), (i), (j).

E. Obtaining Credit

Unless the court orders otherwise, a trustee authorized to operate a debtor's business may obtain and incur unsecured credit and debt in the ordinary course of business. In order to enhance a debtor's ability to obtain credit throughout the course of a bankruptcy, such credit is treated as a high priority administrative expense, which means it is paid out of the estate's assets before other pre-existing claims. Credit may be obtained and debt incurred other than in the ordinary course of business only upon court authorization after notice and hearing.

If the trustee is unable to obtain credit or incur debt even with the assurance that it will be treated as an administrative expense, the court, after notice and hearing, may authorize additional priority. A postpetition creditor could receive, as an additional priority over competing claims:

- priority over any or all administrative expenses;
- a lien on unencumbered assets of the estate; or,
- a junior lien on property of the estate already subject to a lien.

If a trustee is unable to obtain credit otherwise, and can provide adequate protection to the interest of a pre-existing lien holder, the court, after notice and hearing, may authorize the obtaining of credit or the incurring of debt secured by a senior or equal lien on property of the estate that is already subject to a lien. 11 U.S.C § 364(a)-(d).

F. Executory Contract and Unexpired Leases

A trustee, subject to the court's approval, may assume or reject an executory contract or unexpired lease. This permits the bankruptcy estate to shed obligations which are burdensome and impede the likelihood of a successful reorganization, or conversely, to retain advantageous commitments which will benefit the estate and its creditors.

The Code does not define what constitutes an "executory contract," but the legislative history suggests that "it generally includes contracts on which performance remains due to some extent on both sides."[46]

The trustee's power to assume or reject a contract is conditioned. In order to assume, the trustee must cure any default in the contract or lease (other than a default by virtue of filing in bankruptcy) and provide adequate assurance of future performance if there has been a default. Special forms of "adequate assurance" obtain with respect to shopping center leases when the debtor is a lessee. The trustee is prohibited from assuming or assigning a contract or lease if applicable nonbankruptcy law excuses the other party from performance to someone other than the debtor, unless the other party consents.

The trustee must assume or reject within specified time frames. In a liquidation case, the trustee must assume within 60 days (or within an additional 60 days if the court, for cause, extends the time). If not, the contract is deemed rejected. In a reorganization case, the time limit is not fixed, although a party to the contract may request the court to specify a time by which the trustee must make a determination.

The Code invalidates bankruptcy clauses in executory contracts which purport to automatically terminate the contract or lease in the event of bankruptcy. Likewise, the trustee may assign the contract, notwithstanding a contrary provision within it, if assignment is permissible under applicable nonbankruptcy law.

Special provisions govern unexpired leases of real property of the debtor in which the debtor is the lessor, unexpired leases of personal property in which the debtor is lessee, timeshare interests under a timeshare plan in which the debtor is the seller,[47] contracts for the sale of property in which the debtor is seller, executory contracts governing licensing agreements for intellectual property under which the debtor is a licensor, and commitments by a debtor to maintain the capital of an insured depository institution.

When a contract or lease is rejected by the debtor, the other party to the agreement may assert a claim for damages arising from the breach. Such a claim is treated as a prepetition, unsecured claim against the estate. Assumption of the contract is an act of administration of the estate, and the expenses and liabilities connected therewith are high priority expenses of administration. 11 U.S. C. § 365.

---

[46] H.Rept. 95-595, supra note 16 at 347.

[47] The rights of lessees and timeshare buyers as creditors were strengthened pursuant to amendments in § 205 of the 1994 Reform Act, supra note 25.

G. Termination of a Debtor's Utility Service

A utility may not discontinue service to or discriminate against the debtor solely on the basis of the commencement of a case in bankruptcy, or because a debt owed to the utility was not paid when due prior to the filing. The utility may discontinue service, however, if, within 20 days after the order for relief, the debtor does not furnish adequate assurance of payment in the form of a deposit, or other security, for service after that date. The court, after notice and hearing, may adjust the amount of the deposit or other security necessary to provide adequate assurance. 11 U.S.C. § 366.

IV. THE ESTATE

A. Property of the Estate

The filing of a case under the Code creates a bankruptcy estate composed, in part, of the following property, wherever located:

- all legal or equitable interests of the debtor in property as of the commencement of the case;
- all interests of the debtor and spouse in community property under debtor control; or liable for an allowable claim against the debtor, or against the debtor and the debtor's spouse, to the extent such interest is liable;
- property interest received or recovered by the trustee from a custodian, an avoided transfer, a setoff, or general partners in a partnership;
- property acquired by the debtor within 180 days of the commencement of the case – by bequest, devise, or inheritance; as a result of a property settlement agreement or a divorce decree; or, as a beneficiary of a life insurance policy or death benefit plan;
- income from estate property, except income from earnings from services performed by an individual debtor after commencement of the case; and
- any property interest acquired by the estate after commencement of the case.

The estate does *not* include:

- any power that the debtor may only exercise for the benefit of an entity other than the debtor;
- any interest of the debtor as a lessee under a lease of nonresidential real property that has terminated under its terms before the filing in bankruptcy, or that expires in the course of the bankruptcy;
- eligibility of a debtor educational institution to participate in programs authorized under the Higher Education Act, or any accreditation status or state licensure of the debtor;
- certain interests in oil and gas production payments;
- certain interests in cash that constitute proceeds of a sale by the debtor of a money order under an agreement with a money order issuer that prohibits the commingling of such proceeds with property of the debtor; or
- an interest in a spendthrift trust where the restriction on transfer is enforceable under applicable nonbankruptcy law.[48]

With the exception of an enforceable spendthrift trust, other terms of agreements, transfer instruments, or applicable nonbankruptcy laws that restrict or condition transfers of a debtor's interest in property, or that condition transfers on financial insolvency, will not prevent property from coming within the bankruptcy estate. 11 U.S.C. § 541.

B. Turnover of Property of the Estate

When a case is commenced, anyone holding estate property – except a custodian[49] – that the trustee may use, sell, or lease, or that the debtor may

---

[48] In Patterson v. Shumate, 112 S. Ct. 2242 (1992), the Supreme Court addressed a question which had divided the courts of appeals and led to confusion and fragmentation in the bankruptcy administration of pensions qualified under the Employee Retirement Income Security Act (ERISA). The Court held that ERISA-qualified pension plans are excludable from a debtor's estate. Hence, they are not available for distribution to creditors.

[49] A "custodian" means –
(A) receiver or trustee of any of the property of the debtor, appointed in a case or proceeding not under the Code;
(B) assignee under a general assignment for the benefit of the debtor's creditors; or
(C) trustee, receiver, or agent under applicable law, or under a contract, that is appointed or authorized to take charge of property of the debtor for the purpose of enforcing a lien against such property, or for the purpose of general administration of such property for the benefit of the debtor's creditors. 11 U.S.C. § 101(11).

exempt from the estate (see *infra*), must deliver it to the trustee and account for such property or its value.

Likewise, anyone owing a debt that is property of the estate and is matured, payable on demand or order, must (except if it may be setoff against a claim against the debtor) pay it over to the trustee. The court may order attorneys, accountants, other persons holding recorded information (i.e., books, records, documents, and other papers related to the debtor's financial affairs, etc.) to disclose such information to the trustee.

There are specified exceptions to the turnover provisions. A life insurance company may continue to make automatic premium loans from property that may otherwise be property of the estate. And, an entity having no actual notice or knowledge of the commencement of a case by the debtor may transfer estate property, or pay a debt owing to the debtor, to a person other than the trustee, with the same effect as if the debtor had not commenced the case. 11 U.S.C. § 542.

C. Turnover of Property by a Custodian

When a custodian of the debtor's property becomes aware of the commencement of a case by or against the debtor, he is prohibited from making any disbursement thereafter, or taking any action (other than an action to preserve the property) in the administration of the property in his custody and is further required to turn over such property, or proceeds thereof, to the trustee, and to file an accounting of his custodianship.

The bankruptcy court must protect all entities to which the custodian became obligated with respect to such property; provide reasonable compensation to the custodian for services rendered; and, surcharge a custodian for improper or excessive disbursements, unless they were approved by a court or were made in accordance with applicable law. The bankruptcy court may, however, excuse compliance with these requirements if the interests of creditors and equity security holders would be better served by permitting a custodian to continue in possession of the property. 11 U.S.C. § 543.

D. The Trustee's Avoidance Powers

Many provisions in the Bankruptcy Code permit the trustee to nullify or "avoid" prepetition transfers from the debtor to others, including certain liens. The purpose of requiring creditors in specified situations to disgorge monies received from the debtor prior to the bankruptcy is to maximize the bankruptcy estate to ensure equitable distribution among all creditors. Constraints on the trustee's avoidance powers are necessary to protect normal commercial transactions. Although the provisions governing avoidance are extremely complex, they are surveyed below.

1. Trustee as Lien Creditor and as Successor to Certain Creditors and Purchasers

As of the commencement of the case, and without regard to knowledge of the trustee or any creditors, and regardless of whether such creditor or purchaser exists, the trustee has the rights and powers of, or may avoid any property transfer or obligation of the debtor that is voidable by:

- a creditor on a simple contract with a judicial lien on the property;
- a creditor with an unsatisfied writ of execution against property of the debtor;
- bona fide purchasers of debtor's property; and
- an unsecured creditor under applicable law.

This provision is known as the Bankruptcy Code's "strong arm clause."[50] It permits the trustee to assume the attributes of specified hypothetical creditors or bona fide purchases who, under applicable nonbankruptcy law, would be afforded priority in the interest that the trustee seeks to avoid. 11 U.S. C. § 544.

2. Statutory Liens

The trustee may avoid the fixing of a statutory lien to the extent that such lien:

a. first becomes effective against the debtor when –
- a bankruptcy (or other insolvency proceeding not under the Code) is commenced,
- a custodian is appointed,
- the debtor becomes insolvent,

---

[50] H.Rept. 95-595, supra note 16 at 370; Sen. Rep. 95-989, supra note 16 at 85.

- the debtor's financial condition fails to meet a specified standard, or
- an entity other than a statutory lien holder levies execution against the debtor's property;

b. is not perfected or enforced against a bona fide purchaser on the date the case commences, whether the purchaser exists or not;

c. is for rent; or

d. is a lien for distress of rent.

Many of the above-described liens are created under state law to establish priorities for distribution consistent with state plans for insolvency. These priorities have *not* been incorporated into the federal scheme embodies in the Code. 11 U.S.C. § 545.

3. *Limitations on Avoiding Power*

The trustee's rights and powers under certain of the avoiding powers are limited.

The use of such power with respect to statutory liens, preferences, fraudulent transfers and obligations, and as a lien creditor, is subject to a general statutory limitation of the later of two (2) years after the case is filed or one (1) year after the first trustee's appointment under chapter 7, 11, 12, or 13, if this occurs before the case is closed or dismissed, whichever occurs first.

If, under generally applicable law as of the date of the filing of the petition, an interest holder against whom the trustee would have rights (as a lien creditor, or with respect to statutory liens and post-petition transactions) still has the opportunity to perfect, or to maintain or continue perfection of, his lien against an intervening interest holder, then he may perfect his interest against the trustee. If the generally applicable law requires seizure of the property to accomplish perfection and the property has not been seized, then perfection is by notice to the trustee instead.

The trustee may not avoid the seller's right or reclamation if the right asserted was created by statute or common law; the debtor received the goods while insolvent; and, the seller made written demand for reclamation with 10 days after debtor's receipt of the goods (or, if the 10 days expire after the commencement of the case, before 20 days after receipt of such goods by the debtor).

In a chapter 11 case, the court may, on motion, permit the trustee to return goods shipped to the debtor by the creditor before the commencement of the case, and the creditor may offset the purchase price of such goods against any prepetition claim of the creditor.

The Code places additional restraints upon a trustee's avoiding powers when the debtor operates specified businesses, e.g., grain storage facility, fish processing facility, commodity broker, forward contract merchant, stockbroker, swap agreement participants, financial institution or securities clearing agency. 11 U.S.C. § 546.

4. Preferences

A "preference," in essence, is a prebankruptcy transaction which has the effect of favoring one creditor over others.[51] In the absence of the Code's provisions which permit a trustee to avoid such transactions, preferences – like other avoidable transfers – might otherwise be perfectly valid transactions. In order to facilitate the Code policy of "equality of distribution," the trustee may avoid a transfer of property of the debtor if it (1) was made for the benefit of a creditor, (2) on account of an antecedent debt, (3) while the debtor was insolvent, (4) within 90 days before the date of the filing of the petition[52] or between 90 days and one year before the filing of the petition if the creditor was an insider, and (5) enables the creditor to receive more than he would otherwise receive if the debtor's estate were in liquidation or were otherwise distributed under the Code.

Among the transactions that are excluded from attack as a preference and which the trustee may not avoid are:

---

[51] "A preference is a transfer that enables a creditor to receive payment of a greater percentage of his claim against the debtor than he would have received if the transfer had not been made and he had participated in the distribution of the assets of the bankrupt estate. The purpose of the preference section [11 U.S.C. § 547] is two-fold. First, by permitting the trustee to avoid prebankruptcy transfers that occur within a short period before bankruptcy, creditors are discouraged from racing to the courthouse to dismember the debtor during his slide into bankruptcy. The protection thus afforded the debtor often enables him to work his way out of a difficult financial situation through cooperation with all of his creditors. Second, and more important, the preference provisions facilitate the prime bankruptcy policy of equality of distribution among creditors of the debtor. Any creditor that received a greater payment than others of his class is required to disgorge so that all may share equally." H.Rept. 95-595, supra note 16 at 177-78.

[52] For the purposes of calculating time, a transfer made by check is deemed to occur on the date the check is honored by the drawee bank, not the date when it is presented to the creditor. Barnhill v. Johnson, 111 S. Ct. 2150 (1992).

- a transfer which is intended to be and is in fact a contemporaneous exchange for new value (money or money's worth in goods, services, or new credit) given to the debtor;
- a transfer made according to ordinary business terms in payment of a debt incurred by the debtor in the ordinary course of business or financial affairs of the debtor and the transferee;[53]
- a transfer that creates a security interest securing new value in property acquired by the debtor that meets specified conditions and is perfected on or before 20 days after the debtor receives possession of the property;
- a transfer to or for the benefit of a creditor, to the extent that, after such transfer, the creditor gave "new value" to or for the benefit of the debtor and such "new value" is not secured by an otherwise unavoidable security interest; and on account of which the debtor did not make an otherwise unavoidable transfer to the creditor;
- a transfer that creates a perfected security interest in inventory or a receivable or the proceeds of either, except to the extent that the aggregate of all such transfers to the transferee caused a reduction, as of the date of filing of the petition and to the prejudice of other creditors holding unsecured claims, of any amount by which the debt secured by such security interest exceeded the value of all security interests for such debt on the later of specified dates;
- a transfer that is the fixing of a statutory lien that is not avoidable under the Code;
- a transfer which is a bona fide payment to a spouse or former spouse for alimony, maintenance or child support; or
- a transfer in a case filed by an individual debtor whose debts are primarily consumer debts, if the aggregate value of all property that constitutes or is affected by such transfer is less than $600.

The trustee has the burden of proving the avoidability of a transfer which is generally avoidable under this section, while the creditor or party in interest against whom recovery is sought has the burden of proving that the transfer is nonavoidable. 11 U.S.C. § 547.

---

[53] Payments on long-term debt, as well as those on short-term debt, may qualify for the ordinary course of business exception. This interpretation of the statute, established in Union Bank v. Wolas, 112 S. Ct. 527 (1991), overruled a large body of case law holding to the contrary.

5. Fraudulent Transfers and Obligations

Fraudulent transfers and obligations basically fall in two categories – those made with intent to hinder, delay or defraud creditors, and those made while the debtor is insolvent (or which render the debtor insolvent) where the exchange if for less than reasonably equivalent value.[54]

The trustee may avoid any transfer or obligation incurred by the debtor within one year prior to the commencement of the case if the debtor voluntarily or involuntarily:

- made such transfer or incurred such obligation with actual intent to hinder, delay, or defraud an existing or future creditor;
- received less than a reasonably equivalent value in exchange for such transfer and obligation and (a) was insolvent on the date of such transfer or obligation; (b) was, or was about to engage in business or a transaction for which his remaining property was an unreasonably small capital; or, (c) intended to incur, or believed the debtor would incur debts beyond his ability to repay at maturity.

The trustee of a partnership debtor may avoid transfers and obligations incurred by the debtor, within one year prior to commencement of the case to a general partner in the debtor if the debtor was insolvent on the date of such transfer, or was made so because of it.

However, so long as a transfer voidable under any of the above is not also voidable by the trustee as a lien creditor, or as a voidable statutory lien or preference, than a transferee or obligee who takes for value and in good faith (i.e. absence of actual intent to defraud) has a lien on the interest transferred, may retain the lien transferred, or may enforce any obligation incurred, to the extent of the value furnished by the transferee or obligee to the debtor.

This section was amended in 1998 to expressly provide that prepetition contributions of up to 15 percent of a debtor's gross annual income – or more than 15 percent if the contribution is consistent with the debtor's past

---

[54] In a case under the Act of 1898 analyzing the avoidability of exchanges for less than reasonably equivalent value, the United States Court of Appeals for the Fifth Circuit found that the sale of a home at foreclosure for approximately 57.7 percent of its fair market value was not reasonably equivalent and was voidable in bankruptcy by the debtor in possession. Durrett v. Washington National Insurance Co., 621 F.2d 201 (5th Cir. 1980). In 1994, the U.S. Supreme Court, in BFP v. Resolution Trust Corp., 114 S. Ct. 1757, overruled Durrett and resolved a split among the circuit courts by holding that a "reasonably equivalent value" for foreclosed real property is the price in fact received at the foreclosure sale, so long as all the requirements of state foreclosure law have been complied with.

practice – to qualified religious or charitable organizations may not be avoided. Reference is made to the Internal Revenue Code of 1986 for definitions of "charitable contribution" and "qualified religious or charitable" organizations.

6. Postpetition Transactions

As of the commencement of a case – which is usually synonymous with the filing of the petition – the property of the debtor becomes property of the estate. Generally, the trustee may avoid transfers that occur after the filing of the petition which are not expressly authorized by either the Code, without court order, or the court.

In an involuntary case, the trustee may not avoid certain "involuntary gap" transactions, i.e., those which occur between the filing of the petition and the entering of an order for relief, in which the transferee has given new value for the transfer.

Likewise, the trustee may not avoid a transfer of real property to a good faith purchaser if the real property is located outside the county where the case is commenced; if a present, fair equivalent value is paid for the property; if the purchaser does not know of the commencement of the case, and, if a copy of the petition has not been filed in the proper county office for recording real property conveyances before the transfer is perfected against a bona fide purchaser.

Proceedings by a trustee to avoid postpetition transactions may not be commenced after the earlier of two years after the date of transfer or the time the case is closed of dismissed. 11 U.S.C. § 549.

7. Liability of Transferee of Avoided Transfer

When the trustee seeks to avoid a transfer pursuant to the Code, the trustee may recover the property transferred, or, if the court orders, the value of such property not only from the initial transferee, but from others who may have received the property, i.e., any immediate or mediate transferee of the initial transferee. The trustee may not, unless the specific avoidance statute provides otherwise, recover from an immediate or mediate transferee who takes for value without knowledge of the avoidability of the transfer, or who accepts the transfer in good faith.

If a transfer is an avoidable transfer because it was made within 90 days to one year before the filing of the petition; is avoidable under section 547(b); and was made for the benefit of a creditor who at the time of the transfer was an insider, then the trustee may *not* recover under this section from a transferee that is not an insider.

When the trustee may recover property from a good faith transferee, the latter retains a lien on the property recovered to secure the lesser of (a) the cost, to such transferee of any improvement made after the transfer, less the amount of any profit realized by the transferee, and (b) any increase in the value of the property as a result of improvements.

A proceeding against a subsequent transferee must be brought by the earlier of either one year after the avoidance of the transfer on account of which the recovery is sought or the time the case is closed or dismissed. 11 U.S.C. § 550.

E. Postpetition Effect of Security Interest

Under Article 9 of the Uniform Commercial Code, creditors may take security interests in after-acquired property. The Bankruptcy Code, however, governs the effect of such a security interest in postpetition property. As a general rule, if a security agreement is entered into before the commencement of the case, then property acquired by the estate is not subject to the security interest created by a provision in the security agreement extending the security interest to after-acquired property of the debtor.

When the security agreement, by its terms, extends to property acquired by the debtor before commencement of the case and to proceeds, products, offspring, rents or profits of such property, then the security interest may survive the bankruptcy filing to encompass the after-acquired property to the extent provided in the security agreement and by applicable nonbankruptcy law, except a the court, after notice and hearing, may otherwise provide based on the equities of the case.

The Code specifies that a prepetition security agreement for property paid as rents or charges for the use or occupancy of hotel or motel rooms may be treated as encumbered after-acquired property.[55] 11 U.S.C. § 552.

---

[55] The provision addressing proceeds of hotel and motel receipts was added by § 214 of the 1994 Reform Act and was intended to resolve fragmented case law addressing the issue.

F. Setoff

A setoff occurs when there are two debts which arise out of separate transactions, one owed from the debtor and one owed to the debtor, and the party who owes the debt to the debtor reduces the debt to account for that which the debtor owes. Although a setoff may appear to be the type of transaction which is avoidable by a trustee, the Code generally permits it.

Subject to two exceptions and three general restrictions or prohibitions, the Code does not affect creditor's right under applicable nonbankruptcy law to offset prepetition debts owing by him to the debtor. The exceptions to the right of setoff are the automatic stay and the right of the trustee to use, sell, or lease estate property that is subject to a right of setoff. Offset is not allowed:

- if the creditor's claim is not allowed;
- if the claim was transferred to the creditor by someone other than the debtor after commencement of the case, or after 90 days before the commencement of the case, and while the debtor was insolvent.
- if the debt owed to the debtor by the creditor was incurred by the creditor after 90 days before the commencement of the case, while the debtor was insolvent, and for the purpose of obtaining a right of setoff against the debtor.

Subject to certain exceptions, when an offset occurs prior to the commencement of a case, the trustee may recover the setoff to the extent that any "insufficiency," i.e., any amount by which a claim against the debtor exceeds a mutual debt owing to the debtor by the holder of such claim, exists on the later of 90 days before commencing the case, or the first date during such 90 days on which there is an insufficiency. 11 U.S.C. § 553.

G. Abandonment of Property of the Estate

After notice and hearing, the trustee may abandon any property of the estate that is burdensome to the estate or that is of inconsequential value to the estate.[56] A party in interest may request the court to order the trustee to abandon any property of the estate that is burdensome. 11 U.S.C. § 554.

---

[56] A trustee may not abandon property in contravention of state laws reasonably designed to protect the public health and safety. Hence, a chapter 7 debtor would not be permitted to

V. CREDITORS AND CLAIMS

A. Filing of Proofs of Claims

A creditor or an indenture trustee may file a proof of claim. An equity security holder may file a proof of interest. 11 U.S.C. § 501. This requirement is permissive only, and does not require filing of a proof of claim by any creditor. The debtor is generally responsible for filing a schedule of debt and creditors. However, when a debt is incorrectly listed, or when a creditor with a lien is undersecured and asserts a claim for the balance of the debt owed him, this section facilitates filing.

If a creditor fails to file a claim, then the debtor, trustee, or anyone who is liable to the creditor with the debtor (i.e., a codebtor, surety, guarantor, etc.) may file a proof of claim.

All unsecured creditors, except those holding claims entitled to administrative priority, and equity security holders must file a proof of claim if they wish to be eligible to receive a distribution under chapters 7 and 13. In a chapter 11 case, the debtor's schedule of liabilities is adequate unless the creditor takes issue with the amount of the claim, or unless it is not listed, or is listed as disputed, contingent or unliquidated. In a chapter 7 liquidation or chapter 13 reorganization, the proof of claim must be filed by nongovernmental creditors within 90 days after the first date set for the meeting of creditors; in chapter 11 reorganizations, the court sets the date for filing proofs of claim. Bankruptcy Rules 3002, 3003.

B. Allowance of Claims or Interests

When proof of a claim or interest is properly filed, it is deemed allowed unless a party in interest objects. After notice and a hearing, the amount of a disputed claim is determined by the court.

The Code expressly disallows many types of claims. Among those which are disallowed is a claim which:

- is unenforceable against the debtor or his property for any reason other than because it is contingent or unmatured;

---

abandon a toxic, PCB-contaminated oil storage facility in violation of state and federal environmental law. Midlantic National Bank v. New Jersey Department of Environmental Protection, 474 U.S. 494 (1986).

- is for unmatured interest;
- is a property tax claim and the amount due exceeds the value of the estate's interest in the property;
- is for the services of an insider or attorney and exceeds the reasonable value of such services;
- is an unmatured and nondischargeable claim for alimony, maintenance or support to a spouse and children under a divorce decree, separation agreement, or property settlement agreement;
- is a damage claim arising out of a lease termination and, without acceleration, it exceeds the greater of the reserved rental for one year, or fifteen percent, not to exceed three years, of the remaining lease term following the earlier of the date of filing and the date or repossession or surrender of the property, plus the unpaid rent due, without acceleration, under the lease;
- is for damages by an employee arising out of termination of an employment contract which exceed one year's compensation plus any unpaid compensation due under the contract;
- results from a reduction, due to late payment, of an otherwise applicable credit available to the debtor in connection with an employment tax on wages, salaries or commissions earned from the debtor;
- proof of such claim is not timely filed, except as authorized elsewhere in the Code or Bankruptcy Rules, except that the claim of a government unit is timely if it is filed within 180 days after the order for relief;
- is a claim of a claimant who has received a voidable transfer unless the claimant has paid the amount or turned over the property received.

Contingent and unliquidated claims which cannot be fixed or liquidated without delaying the administration of the case may be estimated.[57]

Certain types of claims which may be allowed or disallowed are treated as prepetition claims even thought hey may arise after the filing of the petition. These include claims arising in the ordinary course of the debtor's business after the commencement of the case but before the order for relief is entered in an involuntary case; claims arising from the rejection of an

---

[57] The estimation of personal injury claims for purposes of determining the feasibility of reorganization is often undertaken in chapter 11 cases involving mass tort liability. See,

executory contract or unexpired lease; and specified claims concerning the recovery of property and taxes.

A claim that has been allowed or disallowed may be reconsidered for cause. 11 U.S.C. § 502.

C. Allowance for Administrative Expenses

Claimants may file a request for payment of an administrative expense. Administrative expenses are extremely important because they are "high priority claims" which are paid first out of the debtor's assets. They may be paid prior to or upon confirmation of a reorganization plan, or upon distribution of the estate's assets in a liquidation. Payment of administrative expenses requires notice and hearing. Allowable administrative expenses include:

- the actual, necessary costs and expenses of preserving the estate, including wages, salaries, or commissions for services rendered after the commencement of the case;
- certain taxes incurred by the estate, e.g., taxes attributable to an excessive allowance of a tentative carryback adjustment that the estate received, whether the taxable year to which the adjustment related ended before or after the commencement of the case, including any fine, penalty, or reduction in credit relating to taxes entitled to administrative relief;
- compensation and reimbursement of trustees, examiners, and professional persons employed by the estate. Persons rendering professional services must obtain court approval;
- actual necessary expenses of a creditor who, after court approval, recovers property for the benefit of the estate; prosecutes a criminal offense relating to the case, or to the debtor's property of business; parties, including certain creditors' committees, who make a substantial contribution in a case under chapter 9 or 11; and, the actual and necessary expenses of a chapter 11 committee member and those of a superseded custodian;
- reasonable compensation for professional services rendered by an accountant or attorney, and their actual, necessary expenses;

E.g., A. H. Robins Co., Inc. v. Piccinin, 788 F.2d 994, 1011-1014 (4th Cir. 1986); In Re UNR Industries, Inc., 45 B.R. 322, 326-37 (N.D. Ill. 1984).

- reasonable compensation of an indenture trustee; and
- certain fees and mileage.

11 U.S.C. § 503.

D. Sharing of Compensation

With two exceptions, the sharing of compensation (i.e. fee splitting) among trustees, examiners, professionals, attorneys and accountants is prohibited. Partners and associates in the same professional association are excepted, as are attorneys for petitioning creditors that join in a petition commencing an involuntary case. 11 U.S.C. § 504.

E. Determination of Tax Liability

The court may determine the amount or legality of any tax, any fine, or any penalty relating to tax, whether or not previously assessed, paid, or contested. The bankruptcy court may not make such a determination with respect to taxes when the issues have been adjudicated by an administrative or judicial tribunal before the commencement of the case.

Nor may the court determine the right of the estate to a tax refund unless at least 120 days have passed since the trustee properly requested such refund, or, after such time, the governmental unit has not made a determination with respect to the refund request.

The trustee may request a determination of any unpaid tax liability of the estate incurred during the administration of the case by submitting a tax return and a request for such a determination to the government. Upon payment of the tax due, or, unless the government notifies the trustee of its intent to examine the return and actually does so within specified time frames, the trustee and debtor will be discharged from any liability with respect to such tax. 11 U.S.C. § 505.

F. Determination of Secured Status

The Code distinguishes secured from unsecured claims. A secured creditor is secured only to the extent of the value of the property securing the creditor's claim. To the extent that a lien secures a claim that is not allowed, it is void. The distinction between secured and unsecured is particularly important to the *undersecured* creditor, i.e., a creditor whose secured collateral is worth less than the amount of his claim. An undersecured creditor's claim is bifurcated – it is an allowed secured claim to the extent of the value of the collateral, and an unsecured claim for the balance of the allowed claim.[58] The same treatment applies to a creditor who has a right to offset a mutual debt owing to the debtor, i.e., he will have an allowed secured claim to the extent of the setoff and an allowed unsecured claim for the balance.

An oversecured creditor, that is, one whose collateral is worth more than the amount of the claim, will be allowed to receive interest on his claim and reasonable fees (including attorney fees), costs, or other charges provided under the agreement which is the basis for the claim. The trustee, however, may recover from the collateral the reasonable and necessary costs of preserving or disposing of such property to the extent that any benefit inures to the creditor. 11 U.S.C. § 506.

G. Priorities in Distribution

The Code establishes priorities for the distribution of unsecured claims which may be divided into two categories – priority and nonpriority. Nonpriority unsecured claims will be paid only after payment of priority claims. Unfortunately, there is often little left in a bankruptcy estate for distribution to nonpriority unsecured creditors who may therefore receive only a scant percentage of the amount due. Although these priorities may be more important in a liquidation, or in reorganizations when a debtor's business ceases to operate, a reorganization plan must provide for unsecured creditors in ways consistent with the distributions contemplated under the statute.[59]

- First priority is accorded to administrative expenses of the estate;

---

[58] In Dewsnup v. Timm, 112 S. Ct. 773 (1992), the U.S. Supreme Court held that 506(d) which voids any liens to the extent it is not an "allowed secured claim," cannot be used by a chapter 7 debtor to "strip down" an undersecured creditor's mortgage lien to the judicially determined value of the collateral, even though § 506(a) states than an "allowed claim" is "secured" only to the extent of the collateral's value.

[59] Pursuant to amendments effected by the 1994 Reform Act, monetary amounts for priorities will be adjusted automatically at three-year intervals to reflect changes in the Consumer Price Index. 11 U.S.C. § 104(b).

- Second priority goes to "involuntary gap" creditors, i.e., creditors whose claims arise in the ordinary course of the debtor's business or financial affairs after the filing of an involuntary petition but before either a trustee is appointed or an order for relief is entered;
- Third priority is designated for unsecured claims for wages, salaries, or commissions, but only to the extent of $4,300 for each individual, including vacation, severance and sick leave pay earned by an individual or corporation within 90 days before the date of filing or the date of the cessation of the debtor's business, whichever occurs first; or, for sales commissions earned by an individual or by a corporation with only one employee acting as an independent contractor in the sale of goods or services for the debtor;[60]
- Fourth priority is similar to the third but governs unsecured claims for contributions to an employee benefit plan arising from services rendered within 180 days before the filing or cessation of the debtor's business, but only to the extent of the number of employees covered by each such plan multiplied by $4,300 less the aggregate amount paid to such employees under the third priority, plus the aggregate amount paid by the estate on behalf of such employees to any other employee benefit plan;
- Fifth priority goes to the unsecured claims of persons engaged in the production or raising of grain against a debtor who owns or operates a grain storage facility, and of persons engaged as a United States fisherman against a debtor who operates a fish produce storage or processing facility, but only to the extent of $4,300 for each such individual;
- Sixth priority is for allowed unsecured claims of individuals, to the extent of $1,950 for each individual, arising from the deposit, before the commencement of the case, of money for the purchase, lease or rental of property, or the purchase of services for personal, family of household use that were not delivered or provided;
- Seventh priority – with no monetary limits – was added in 1994 and goes to allowed claims for debts to a spouse, former spouse, or

---

[60] Priority for sales commissions of independent contractors was added by § 207 of the 1994 Reform Act. The contractor must have made the sales in the ordinary course of the debtor's business and must have earned 75% of total earnings in the year preceding the filing in sales of the debtor's goods or services.

child of the debtor, for alimony or support, in connection with a separate agreement, divorce decree, or property settlement;[61]

- Eighth priority addresses unsecured claims by governmental units for a wide range of taxes, including income taxes, property taxes, withholding taxes, employment taxes, excise taxes,[62] customs duties, and an erroneous tax refund or credit; and

- Ninth priority – with no monetary limits – is for allowed unsecured claims based upon a commitment by the debtor to a Federal depository institutions regulatory agency to maintain the capital of an insured depository institution.

With respect to secured creditors, the Code grants a "super" priority to creditors for losses incurred by a secured creditor arising when it is determine that he received inadequate protection of his interests during the automatic stay, or in the trustee's use, sale or lease of estate property, and in credit transactions with a trustee authorized to operated a debtor's business. 11 U.S.C. § 507.

An additional "super" priority exists for administrative expenses incurred after conversion of a chapter 11, 12, or 13 case to a chapter 7 liquidation. 11 U.S. C. § 726(b).

H. Claims of Codebtors; Subordination

A codebtor (i.e., surety, guarantor, or co-maker) who pays a claim is subrogated to the rights of the creditor to the extent of the payment. The court is required to subordinate the claim of a surety or codebtor of an obligation to a creditor of the estate, unless the creditor has been paid in full. 11 U.S.C. § 509.

---

[61] Section 304 of the 1994 Reform Act makes widespread amendments raising the level of protection in bankruptcy accorded to alimony and support payments. See also, 11 U.S.C. §§ 362, 522, 523, and 547 governing automatic stays, exemptions, dischargeability and avoidable transactions.

[62] A provision in the Internal Revenue Code, 26 U.S.C. § 4971(a), imposes a 10 percent "tax" on an accumulated funding deficiency from an annual contribution to specified pension plans. The Government filed a proof of claim for tax liability, arguing that it was entitled to priority as an "excise tax." The U.S. Supreme Court held that the claim was not entitled to priority as an "excise tax" despite the fact that it was so characterized under the Internal Revenue Code. For bankruptcy purposes, the claim constituted a penalty to be dealt with as an ordinary, unsecured claim. Hence, the Court will examine whether a particular exaction called a "tax" in the statute creating it is also one for bankruptcy purposes. United States v. Reorganized CR&I Fabricators of Utah, 116 S. Ct. 2106 (1996).

A subordination agreement is enforceable in bankruptcy to the same extent that such agreement is enforceable under applicable nonbankruptcy law. The Code also recognizes principles of equitable subordination, which generally hold that a claim or interest may be subordinated only if its holder is guilty of inequitable conduct. The bankruptcy court makes a determination of equitable subordination on a case-by-case basis.[63] 11 U.S.C. § 510.

VI. THE DEBTOR'S DUTIES AND BENEFITS

A. Basic Duties

The Code specified five duties of the debtor that pertain to all cases. Although it is by no means exhaustive of all of the debtor's responsibilities in bankruptcy, the debtor must:

- file a list of creditors with the court, and, unless the court orders otherwise, a schedule of assets and liabilities and a statement of the debtor's financial affairs;
- if the debtor's debts include consumer debts which are secured by property of the estate and a petition is filed under chapter 7, the debtor must file a statement of his intention to retain or surrender the property and, if applicable, specify property that is claimed as exempt, property that he intends to redeem, or debts that he intends to reaffirm;
- cooperate with the trustee, if one is serving;
- surrender to the trustee all estate property and any recorded information (i.e. books, papers, records, documents relating to estate property); and
- appear at any hearing on discharge

11 U.S.C. § 521.

---

[63] Overruling a court of appeals' finding that postpetition, nonpecuniary loss tax penalty claims are "'susceptible to subordination' by their very 'nature[,]'" the U.S. Supreme Court held that "Congress could have, but did not, deny noncompensatory, postpetition tax penalties the first priority given to other administrative expenses, and bankruptcy courts may not take it upon themselves to make that categorical determination under the guise of equitable subordination." United States v. Noland, 116 S. Ct. 1524 (1994). See also, United States v. Reorganized CF&I Fabricators of Utah, 116 S. Ct. 2106 (1996).

B. Exemptions; Waiver of Exemptions

A legal treatise observes that "[f]ew people would voluntarily take any legal action which meant the surrender of so much of their possessions as to leave them destitute and virtually helpless."[64] Hence, when an individual debtor's assets are liquidated, the law permits him or her to retain a certain minimum of money and property necessary to realize a "fresh start."

Although it would be within Congress' authority to establish a uniform set of bankruptcy exemptions which would be finding upon the sates by virtue of the Supremacy Clause, the Code does not do so. For policy considerations, including deference to states' rights, Congress permits not just that the debtor make an election between federal and state created exemptions,[65] but permits the states to deny debtors the use of federal exemptions as well. Consequently, even though there is a significant variance between the states in the generosity of their exemptions, more than half have enacted laws that deny debtors the use of federal exemptions.[66]

When the debtor's state of domicile has *not* enacted legislation which precludes a debtor from electing federal exemptions, the following are available:[67]

- the debtor's aggregate interest, not to exceed $16,150, in real or personal property that the debtor uses as a residence, or in a burial plot for the debtor or a dependent;
- the debtor's interest, not to exceed $2,575, in a motor vehicle;
- the debtor's interest, not to exceed $425, in any one item or $8,624 in aggregate value, in household furnishings, household goods, wearing apparel, appliances, books, animals, crops, or musical instruments, that are held for personal or family use of the debtor;
- the debtor's aggregate interest, not to exceed $1,075, in jewelry held primarily for the personal use of the debtor;

---

[64] 2 Cowans Bankr. Law and Practice § 8.1 (6th Ed. 1994).

[65] In joint cases, or in individual cases where the estates of a husband and wife are administered jointly, debtors may elect either state or federal exemptions – if the latter are permitted in the debtors' state – but one debtor may not elect state exemptions and another elect federal. This practice, known as "stacking" exemptions, was stopped pursuant to 1984 amendments to 11 U.S.C. § 522(b).

[66] 2 Cowans, supra at § 8.2.

[67] Pursuant to amendments effected by the 1994 Reform Act, monetary amounts for exemptions will be adjusted automatically at three-year intervals to reflect the change in the Consumer Price Index. 11 U.S.C. § 104(b).

- the debtor's aggregate interest in any property, not to exceed $850, plus up to $8,075 of any unused amount of the exemption for housing above;
- the debtor's aggregate interest, not to exceed $1,625, in any implement, professional books, or tools of the trade of the debtor;
- any unmatured life insurance contract owned by the debtor;
- the debtor's aggregate interest, not to exceed $8,625, in any accrued dividend under, or loan value of, any unmatured life insurance contract under which the insured is the debtor;
- professionally prescribed health aids;
- the debtor's right to receive social security benefits, unemployment compensation, public assistance benefits, veterans' benefits, disability, illness or unemployment benefits, alimony and support to the extent reasonably necessary;
- benefits under certain pension, profit sharing, stock bonuses, annuity or similar plan or contract, to the extent necessary for the support of the debtor;
- the debtor's right to receive property traceable to an award under a crime victim's reparation law; a payment on account of a wrongful death of an individual of whom the debtor was a dependent, to the extent reasonably necessary for the support of the debtor; a personal injury award not exceeding $16,150 for actual compensation (not including pain and suffering); and, payment in compensation for loss of future earnings, to the extent reasonably necessary for support.

In states where federal elections are not permitted, the debtor would be limited to his exemptions under applicable state and nonbankruptcy federal statutes.[68] In addition, property held by the debtor which would be exempt from process under applicable state nonbankruptcy law, including property held as a tenant by the entirety or joint tenant, may be exemptible.

Exempt property is exempt from *all* prepetition claims, including nondischargeable ones, with specified exceptions. They include debts for certain nondischargeable taxes, alimony, maintenance and child support, debts secured by certain nonavoidable liens, and specified debts owned by a

---

[68] Examples of federal nonbankruptcy exemptions include veterans' pensions, life insurance and disability benefits, 38 U.S. C. § 3101(a); Social Security benefits, 42 U.S.C. § 407; Federal Civil Service disability, death, and retirement benefits, 5 U.S.C. §§ 8130, 8346(a); Military Survivor Benefit Plan Annuities, 10 U.S. C. § 1450(i); and, Servicemen and Veteran's group life insurance benefits, 38 U.S.C. § 770(g).

financial institution-affiliated party to a federal depository institutions regulatory agency.

A debtor may be permitted to avoid certain judicial and nonpossessory, nonpurchase money liens which might otherwise impair a claim to exemptible property. These are liens created by the courts or by the debtor's consent which encumber property of the debtor that would be exemptible in bankruptcy *but for* the subject lien.[69]

In 1991, the Supreme Court held that judicial liens can be eliminated in bankruptcy even though a state has defined exempt property in such a way as to specifically exclude property encumbered by a judicial or nonpossessory, nonpurchase money lien.[70] In other words, even if state law honored the encumbrance against property which would ordinarily be exemptible, the debtor nonetheless may avoid the subject liens. The 1994 amendments to the Code carve out a limited exception to this principle. In cases where the debtor is limited to, or has chose, state law exemptions, if state law honors judicial or consensual liens on certain property that might otherwise be claimed as exempt, namely, implements, professional books, or tools of the trade, the debtor may *not* avoid the security interest to the extent that the value of such property is in excess of $5,000.

A lien is considered to "impair" an exemption to the extent that the sum of the lien, all other liens on the property, and the amount of the exemption that the debtor could claim if there were no liens on the property exceeds the value that the debtor's interest in the property would have in the absence of any liens.

Waiver. A debtor's waiver of an exemption in favor of an unsecured claim is unenforceable. Since a debtor is permitted to exempt property recovered by the trustee pursuant to his avoiding power, or recovered pursuant to a setoff, a waiver of those rights against property which may otherwise be exempted may also be unenforceable. 11 U.S.C. § 522.

C. Discharge

A "discharge" in bankruptcy affords the debtor a "fresh start." If a discharge is granted, the debtor's obligation to pay prepetition debt is

---

[69] Section 303 of the 1994 Reform Act, supra note 25, prohibits the debtor from avoiding a judicial lien in connection with a separation agreement or divorce decree that secures a debt to a spouse, former spouse, or child of the debtor for alimony, maintenance or child support.

[70] Owen v. Owen, 111 S. Ct. 1833 (1991).

extinguished. The manner of obtaining a discharge, and its effect, varies between individuals and businesses. The Code specified what types of debt are dischargeable and nondischargeable, and the latter category includes many debts which the court will examine and decide upon on a case-by-case basis. A discharge voids any judgment to the extent that it is a determination of the personal liability of the debtor with respect to a prepetition debt, and operates as an injunction against the commencement or continuation of all legal and nonlegal actions to offset, recover, or collect a debt from the debtor or his property, whether or not discharge of such debt is waived.[71] 11 U.S.C. § 524(a).

In 1994, the Code was amended to ratify the approach taken by the Johns-Manville Corp., which established a trust under the auspices of the bankruptcy court to satisfy present and future personal injury claims against it based on exposure to asbestos-containing products. The Code expressly authorizes the creation of a trust to pay future claims for an asbestos-related disease, coupled with an injunction to prevent future claimants from suing the debtor 11 U.S.C. § 524(g).

D. Reaffirmation Agreements

Whether or not discharge has been waived, a reaffirmation by the debtor of a dischargeable debt is enforceable only to any extent enforceable under nonbankruptcy law and only if the agreement is made before discharge, and is not rescinded by the debtor within thirty days after it becomes enforceable.

In the case of an individual who enters into a reaffirmation agreement, the court will scrutinize the agreement to determine that the debtor has entered into it with knowledge of his rights under Title 11 and with an understanding of its consequences. If the debtor was not represented by an attorney during the course of negotiating a pre-discharge reaffirmation agreement, the court must approve the agreement as (i) not imposing an undue hardship on the debtor and (ii) being in the best interest of the debtor.[72]

---

[71] "The injunction is to give complete effect to the discharge and to eliminate any doubt concerning the effect of the discharge as a total prohibition on debt collection efforts. This paragraph has been expanded over a comparable provision in [the Bankruptcy Act of 1898] to cover any act to collect, such as dunning by telephone or letter, or indirectly through friends, relatives, or employers, harassment, threats of repossession, and the like." H.Rept. 95-595, supra note 16 at 365-366.

[72] Sears, Roebuck, & Co. entered into a multimillion dollar settlement stemming from a widespread failure to file reaffirmation agreements with the bankruptcy courts. As a result

Nothing contained with the provisions addressing reaffirmation agreements is intended to prevent a debtor from voluntarily repaying any debt that is otherwise dischargeable under the Code. 11 U.S.C. § 524(c)(d)&(e).

E. Exceptions to Discharge

Certain debts are excepted from discharge under chapters 7, 11, and 13;[73] the dischargeability of other types of debt must be determined by the court. Among those obligations which are excepted from discharge are:

- a customs duty or tax (income, property, employment, etc.) with respect to which a return was not filed; was filed after the due data and after two years before the date of filing the petition; was fraudulently prepared for the purpose of willfully evading or defeating the tax;
- debts which are not listed or scheduled by the debtor identifying the creditor so as to permit him to timely file a proof of claim (unless the creditor has actual knowledge of the case);
- debts to a spouse, former spouse, or child of the debtor, for alimony to, maintenance for, or support of such spouse or child, or under a property settlement agreement;[74]
- a debt of a fine, penalty, or forfeiture payable to a governmental unit that is not compensation for actual pecuniary loss, other than a tax penalty relating to a tax that is otherwise dischargeable, or imposed with respect to a transaction or event that occurred three years before the bankruptcy filing;[75]

---

of an investigation by the Boston Office of the U.S. Trustee, Sears identified more than 146,000 customers nationwide who signed invalid reaffirmation agreements between January 1992 and April 1997. 9 NVA Bankr. Law Reporter 1089 (Sept. 11, 1997).

[73] Chapter 13 has unique discharge provisions which are discussed infra.

[74] A debt may be discharged if it is assigned to another entity either voluntarily or by operation of law, other than an assignment to the Federal government, to a state government, or to a political subdivision of a state. Likewise, to be nondischargeable, debt characterized as child support and alimony must actually be in the nature of alimony, maintenance, or support.

[75] The exception to discharge for fines and penalties includes any condition a state criminal court imposes as part of a criminal sentence, including a restitution obligation imposed as a condition of probation in state criminal proceedings. Hence, restitution payments are nondischargeable even though, unlike traditional fines, payments may be forwarded to the victim and may be calculated by reference to the amount of harm the offender has caused

- a debt for an educational benefit overpayment or loan made, insured, or guaranteed by a governmental unit, or made under a program funded by a governmental unit or a nonprofit institution unless failure to grant a discharge will impose an undue hardship on the debtor and the debtor's dependents;[76]

- a debt which arises from death or personal injury caused by the debtor's operation of a motor vehicle while legally intoxicated;

- a debt that was or could have been listed by the debtor in a prior case under the Bankruptcy Code or its predecessor, the Bankruptcy Act, in which the debtor waived discharge or was denied discharge;

- a debt provided for in any final judicial judgment, order, or consent decree, or issued by a federal depository institutions regulatory agency, or contained in a settlement agreement, arising from any act of fraud or defalcation while the debtor was acting in a fiduciary capacity with respect to a depository institution or insured credit unit;

- a debt arising from malicious or reckless failure to fulfill a commitment by the debtor to a federal depository institutions regulatory agency to maintain the capital of an insured depository institution;

- a debt for any payment of an order of restitution issued under Title 18 of the U.S. Code;[77]

- a debt incurred to a third-party to pay a tax to the United States that would be nondischargeable under the provisions above;[78]

- a debt of a postpetition fee or assessment from the debtor's condominium or cooperative membership association, but only if

---

and thereby represent compensation for actual pecuniary loss. Kelly v. Robinson, 479 U.S. 36 (1986).

[76] Nondischargeability was extended to an educational benefit overpayment made or insured by a governmental unit as well as to "an obligation to repay funds received as an educational benefit, scholarship or stipend" pursuant to amendments in P.L. 101-647, Title XXXVI, §§ 3621, 3631 (Nov. 29, 1990). Prior to amendments in 1998, student loans could be discharged if the loan first became due before seven years before the filing of the petition. P.L. 105-244, § 971 (Oct. 7, 1998).

[77] This exception to discharge was added by § 320934 of the Violent Crime Control and Law Enforcement Act of 1994, P.L. 103-322, 108 Stat. 1796 (Sept. 13, 1994).

[78] This exception to dischargeability was added by § 221 of the Reform Act. It is intended to protect credit card companies to the extent that taxes are paid via credit card and "will facilitate individuals' ability to use their credit cards to pay their Federal taxes." H.Rept. 103-835, 103d Congress, 2d Session 51 (1994).

the fee or assessment is payable for a period during which the debtor physically occupied or rented the dwelling unit;[79]

- a debt for costs, expenses, or a fee imposed by a court for filing a case, motion, complaint, or appeal regardless of an assertion of poverty by the debtor, or the debtor's status as a prisoner;[80]

- a debt owed under state law to a state or municipality that is in the nature of support and is enforceable under part D of title IV of the Social Security Act, 42 U.S.C. § 601 *et seq.*[81]

Certain types of debt *may* be discharged unless, at the request of a creditor to whom the debt is owed, the court, after notice and a hearing, finds the debt to be nondischargeable, namely:[82]

- debts for money, property, service, or credit, to the extent obtained by false pretenses, a false representation, or actual fraud, other than a statement respecting the debtor's financial condition;[83] or, by use of a statement in writing that is materially false with respect to the debtor's financial condition which the creditor reasonably relied on, and that the debtor causes to be made or published with intent to deceive; or, for consumer debts owed to a single creditor aggregating more than $1,075 for "luxury goods or services" incurred by the debtor within sixty days before the order for relief,

---

[79] This exception, also added by the 1994 Reform Act, expressly does not apply to prepetition fees, which presumably remain subject to discharge. H.Rept. 103-835 at 56.

[80] This provision was added by P.L. 104-134, § 804(b), 110 Stat. 1321-74 (April 26, 1996), the Prison Litigation Reform Act. It was apparently intended to discourage habeas corpus litigation.

[81] This exception was added by P.L. 104-193, § 374, 110 Stat. 2255 (August 22, 1996), the Welfare Reform Act. It is intended to make nondischargeable debts incurred by a state for child support that may be advanced by the state absent a court order, or for support rights that may be assigned by a parent to the state for collection against another parent.

[82] When the debtor is an institution-affiliated party, and the creditor is a federal depository institutions regulatory agency acting in its capacity as conservator, receiver, or liquidating agent for an insured depository institution which seeks recovery of a debt arising from fraud, willful injury, or breach of fiduciary duty, it need not specially plead nondischargeability in most circumstances. 11 U.S.C. § 523(c)(2).

[83] In Field v. Mans, 116 S.Ct. 437 (1995), the Supreme Court held that the standard of proof that a creditor must demonstrate in order to except a debt from discharge as a fraudulent representation is not "reasonable reliance," but the less demanding one of justifiable reliance on the representation. And, in Cohen v. De La Cruz, 118 S. Ct. 1212 (1998), the Court held that nondischargeable debts for "actual fraud" may include all liability arising therefrom, including treble damages and attorney's fees.

or cash advances aggregating more than $1,075 obtained by an individual debtor within sixty days before the order for relief.[84]

- debts for fraud or defalcation while acting in a fiduciary capacity, embezzlement, or larceny;

- debts for willful and malicious injury by the debtor to another entity or to the property of another entity; and

- a debt incurred by the debtor in the course of a divorce decree, separation agreement of court order (other than those described above for alimony, maintenance, or support) *unless* the debtor does not have the ability to pay such debt from income or property of the debtor not reasonably necessary to be expended for the maintenance and support of the debtor and the debtor's dependents, and, if the debtor is engaged in a business, for the payment of expenditures necessary for continuation and preservation of such business; or, discharging the debt would result in a benefit to the debtor that outweighs the detrimental consequences to a spouse, former spouse, or child of the debtor.[85]

11 U.S.C. § 523.

F. Protection against Discriminatory Treatment

A governmental unit may not deny, revoke, suspend, or refuse to renew a license, permit, charter, franchise, or other similar grant to a debtor, or condition such grant or discriminate with respect to such grant solely

---

[84] When a creditor requests determination of dischargeability of a consumer debt and the debt is discharged, the court may grant judgment in favor of the debtor for costs and a reasonable attorney's fee for the proceeding if the court finds that the position of the creditor was not substantially justified.

[85] This qualified exception to dischargeability was added by the Bankruptcy Reform Act of 1994. Committee report language indicates that the exception is designed to cover types of property settlements other than those embodied in alimony and support obligations. H.Rept. 103-835 at 54:

In some instances, divorcing spouses have agreed to make payments of marital debts, holding the other spouse harmless from those debts, in exchange for a reduction in alimony payments. In other cases, spouses have agreed to lower alimony based on a larger property settlement. If such "hold harmless" and property settlement obligations are not found to be in the nature of alimony, maintenance or support, they are dischargeable under current law. The nondebtor spouse may be saddled with substantial debt and little or no alimony or support. This [exception to discharge] will make such obligations nondischargeable in cases where the debtor has the ability to pay them and the detriment to the nondebtor spouse from their nonpayment outweighs the benefit to the debtor of discharging such debts.

because a debtor is insolvent prior to, or has filed for protection under the Code; it may not discriminate against, deny, or terminate the employment of, or discriminate with respect to employment against a person solely because the debtor is or has been a debtor under the Bankruptcy Code, or has not paid a debt that is discharged.

No private employer may terminate the employment of, or discriminate with respect to employment against an individual who is or has been a debtor under the Code solely because of the insolvency prior to bankruptcy, the bankruptcy filing, or because the debtor has not paid a debt that is dischargeable or was dischargeable in bankruptcy.[86]

No government unit or private lender may deny a student loan or loan guarantee to an individual on account of the individual having filed in, or received a discharge in bankruptcy.[87] 11 U.S.C. § 525.

This section does not, however, prevent lenders from considering the fact of a bankruptcy when deciding to extend credit. Pursuant to 15 U.S.C. § 1681c, credit reporting agencies may report an individual's action under the Bankruptcy Code for 10 years after the filing of the order for relief or the date of adjudication; the 10 year limit does not apply to credit transactions involving a principal amount of $50,000 or more, the underwriting of life insurance involving a face amount of $50,000 or more, or the employment of an individual a an annual salary of $20,000 or more.

VII. CHAPTER 7 – LIQUIDATION

A. Appointment of a Trustee

A trustee is always appointed to preside over the consolidation and ultimate distribution of the estate in a chapter 7 liquidation.

---

[86] This provision is not exhaustive of the forms of prohibited discrimination. Congress intended to permit the courts to expand upon the rule of Perez v. Campbell, 402 U.S. 637 (1971), which held that a state would frustrate the Congressional policy of a fresh start for a debtor if it were permitted to refuse to renew a drivers license because a tort judgment resulting from an automobile accident had been unpaid as a result of a discharge in bankruptcy. S.Rept. 94-989, supra note 16 at 81.

[87] Added by § 313 of the 1994 Reform Act, "[t]his section clarifies the antidiscrimination provisions of the Bankruptcy Code to ensure that applicants for student loans or grants are not denied those benefits due to a prior bankruptcy." H.Rept. 103-835 at 58.

1. Interim Trustee

Promptly after an order for relief is entered, the U.S. Trustee is directed to appoint an interim trustee. If necessary, the U.S. Trustee may serve as an interim trustee. 11 U.S.C. § 701.

2. Election of a Trustee

At the first meeting of creditors, they may vote to elect one person to serve as trustee if election is requested by creditors who may vote. A creditor may vote only if he (i) holds an allowable, undisputed, fixed, liquidated, unsecured claim that is not entitled to priority, but is entitled to distribution; (ii) does not have an interest materially adverse to the general unsecured creditors; and (iii) is not an insider. A candidate for trustee is elected if general unsecured creditors holding 20% of the amount of such claims actually vote, and if the candidate receives a majority of those votes. The interim trustee serves as the permanent trustee in the case if a trustee is not so elected. 11 U.S.C. § 702.

3. Successor Trustee

If an elected trustee fails to qualify, dies, resigns, or is removed for cause during the case, the creditors may elect another trustee in the manner described above to fill the vacancy.

Pending such election, or if the creditors do not elect a successor trustee, the United States Trustee may appoint an interim or successor trustee, or, if necessary, serve as trustee in the case. 11 U.S.C. § 703.

B. Duties of the Trustee

A chapter 7 trustee must:

- collect and reduce to money the property of the estate and close the estate as expeditiously as is compatible with the best interests of the parties involved;
- be accountable for all property received;
- ensure that the debtor performs his declared intention with respect to property to be retained, surrendered, exempted, or redeemed, and with respect to debts which the debtor intends to reaffirm;
- investigate the debtor's financial affairs;

- if a purpose would be served, examine proofs of claims and object to the allowance of claims that appear to be improper;
- if advisable, oppose the discharge of the debtor;
- unless the court orders otherwise, furnish such information concerning the estate that is requested by a party in interest; if the business of the debtor is authorized to be operated, file with the court, with the U.S. Trustee, and with appropriate governmental tax units, periodic reports and summaries of the operation of such business, including a statement of receipts and disbursements; and
- make a final report and a final account of the administration of the estate with the court and with the U.S. Trustee.

11 U.S.C. § 704.

C. Creditors' Committee

Unsecured creditors entitled to vote for a trustee may also elect a creditors' committee composed of not less than three nor more than eleven creditors. The committee may consult with the trustee or the U.S. Trustee in connection with the administration of the estate, make recommendations respecting the performance of the trustee's duties, and submit to the court or to the U.S. Trustee any question affecting the administration of the estate. 11 U.S.C. § 705.

D. Authorization to Operate Business

If it is consistent with the orderly liquidation of the estate, and in the estate's best interest the court may authorize a trustee to operate the debtor's business for a limited period. 11 U.S.C. § 721.

E. Redemption of Personal Property

The debtor may redeem tangible personal property intended primarily for personal, family, or household use, from a lien securing a dischargeable consumer debt by paying the lienholder the amount of his allowed claim secured by such lien.[88] 11 U.S.C. § 722.

F. Rights of Partnership Trustee against General Partners

This statute provides that each general partner in a partnership debtor is liable to the partnership'' trustee for any deficiency in partnership assets to pay in full all administrative expenses and all claims against the partnership to the extent that the general partner is personally liable under applicable nonbankruptcy law.[89]

The trustee may seek recovery of any deficiency from any general partner who is not a debtor in a bankruptcy case. The court may order the nondebtor partner to indemnify the estate or not to dispose of property pending a determination of the deficiency.

If the aggregate recovered by the trustee from the estates of the general partners exceeds the deficiency, the court, after notice and haring, shall determine an equitable distribution for the surplus which the trustee shall distribute to the estates of the general partners. 11 U.S.C. § 723.

G. Avoidance and Distribution of Certain Liens

The trustee is permitted to avoid a lien that secures a fine, penalty, forfeiture, or multiple, punitive, or exemplary damages claims to the extent that the claim is not compensation for actual pecuniary loss.

The statute also deals with the order of distribution of property upon which there may be an unavoidable tax lien. The Code subordinates payment

---

[88] "The right to redeem extends to the whole of the property, not just the debtor's exempt interest in it. Thus, for example, if a debtor owned a $2,000 car, subject to a $1,200 lien, the debtor could exempt his $800 interest in the car. The debtor is permitted a $1,500 exemption in a car, proposed 11 U.S.C.   522(d)(2) [note: 11 U.S.C. § 522(d)(2) currently permits a $2,400 exemption in an automobile]. This section permits him to pay the holder of the lien $1,200 and redeem the entire car, not just the remaining $700 [sic] of his exemption. The redemption is accomplished by paying the holder of the lien the amount of the allowed claim secured by the lien. The provision amounts to a right of first refusal for the debtor in consumer goods that might otherwise be repossessed." H.Rept. 95-595, supra note 15 at 380-381.

[89] This provision was amended by § 212 of the 1994 Reform Act to clarify "that a partner of a registered limited liability partnership would only be liable in bankruptcy to the extent a partner would be personally liable for a deficiency according to the registered limited liability statute under which the partnership was formed." H.Rept. 103-835, 103d Congress, 2d Session 47 (1994).

of certain tax liens in favor of other interests. Property, or proceeds would first be distributed to a holder of an allowed claim secured by a lien on the property that is senior to the tax lien; second, for administrative expenses and to holders of specified high-priority unsecured claims; third, to the holder of the tax lien; fourth, to the holder of an allowed claim secured by a lien that is junior to the tax lien; fifth, to the holder of the tax lien, if there are still proceeds for distribution; and sixth, to the estate. 11 U.S.C. § 724.

H. Distribution of Property of the Estate

The order for distribution of property of the estate which is not designated as collateral for a secured interest is set forth at 11 U.S.C. § 726, namely:

- in payment of administrative expenses and high-priority unsecured claims set forth at 11 U.S.C. § 507, discussed *supra*;
- to general unsecured creditors whose claims are timely filed (either by the creditor, or a trustee, debtor or codebtor on behalf of the creditor) or are tardily filed because the creditor had no notice or actual knowledge of the case, and proof of such claim is filed in time to permit its payment;
- to general unsecured creditors who tardily file their claim;
- in payment of secured or unsecured allowed claims for a fine, penalty, forfeiture, or for multiple, exemplary, or punitive damages, arising before the earlier of the order for relief or the appointment of a trustee, to the extent that they are not compensation for actual pecuniary loss suffered by the claimholder;
- in payment of post-petition interest (at the legal rate) on any claim above; and
- to the debtor.

Claims within a particular class are to be paid pro rate when there are not enough funds to pay each claimant in full. A superpriority, however, is conferred upon administrative expenses incurred under chapter 7 over administrative expenses which arose in another chapter (i.e., 11, 12, or 13) before it was converted to chapter 7, and over expenses incurred by a custodian in preserving a debtor's property prior to its turnover by the custodian to a trustee.

Community property of the debtor and spouse are segregated and dealt with separately.[90]

I. Discharge

1. Obtaining Discharge

The discharge is at the heart of the "fresh start" for the debtor.[91] The court is required to grant the debtor a discharge in bankruptcy unless one of ten of the following conditions are met:

- the debtor is not an individual;[92] the debtor has, with intent to
- hinder, delay, or defraud a custodial officer of the estate, or a creditor, transferred, removed, destroyed, mutilated or concealed his property within on year before the filing date of the petition; or property of the estate after such filing date; or has permitted such acts to be done;
- the debtor has concealed, destroyed, mutilated, falsified or failed to keep or preserve records, books, documents, papers, etc. from which his financial condition or business transactions might be ascertained – unless the failure is justified under the circumstances;
- the debtor knowingly and fraudulently made a false oath or account; presented a false claim; gave, received, or attempted to obtain money, property, or advantage, for acting or forbearing to act; or, withheld from an officer of the estate any information relating to the debtor's financial affairs;
- the debtor, before determination of a denial of discharge, fails to satisfactorily explain a deficiency of assets to meet his liabilities;
- the debtor refuses to obey lawful court orders (other than one to respond to a material question or to testify); to respond to a material question approved by the court on the ground of the privilege

---

[90] 11 U.S.C. § 726(c) provides for the distribution of the community property. The order of distribution is not substantially different from that discussed above, but provision is made for community claims against the debtor or the debtor's spouse.

[91] H.Rept. 95-595, supra note 16 at 384.

[92] "This is a change from present law [Bankruptcy Act of 1898], under which corporations and partnerships may be discharged in liquidation cases, thought they rarely are. The change in policy will avoid trafficking in corporate shells and in bankruptcy partnerships. 'Individual' includes a deceased individual, so that if the debtor dies during the bankruptcy case, he will nevertheless be released from his debts, and his estate will not be liable for them." Id.

against self-incrimination after the debtor has been granted immunity; to respond to a court approved question on a ground other than a properly invoked privilege against self-incrimination;

- the debtor commits any act specified above or on within one year before the filing of the petition, or during the case, or in connection with another bankruptcy case concerning an insider;
- the debtor has been granted a discharge under chapter 7 or chapter 11 in a case commenced within six years before the filing of the petition;
- the debtor has been granted a discharge under either chapter 12 or 13 in a case commenced within six years before the date of the filing of the petition, unless payments under the reorganization plan totaled at least (i) 100 percent of the allowed unsecured claims in the case, or (ii) 70 percent of such claims and the plan was proposed by the debtor in good faith and was the debtor's best effort; or
- the court approves a written waiver of discharge executed by the debtor after the order for relief is entered. 11 U.S.C. § 727(a).

2. Effect of Discharge

With the exception of debts that are nondischargeable, a chapter 7 discharge, when granted, discharges the debtor from all debts and liability on claims that arose before the date of the order for relief. It is irrelevant whether or not a proof of claim was filed with respect to the debt, and whether or not the claim based on the debt was allowed. 11 U.S.C. § 727(b).

3. Objection To and Revocation of the Debtor's Discharge

The trustee, a creditor, or the U.S. Trustee may ask the court to revoke a discharge if it was obtained through the fraud of the debtor and the requesting party did not know of the fraud until after the discharge was granted. The complaint for revocation must be made within one year of the grant of discharge. Other grounds for revocation are the debtor's having acquired property of the estate, having become entitled to acquire property, and knowingly and fraudulently failing to report the acquisition or entitlement, or to surrender the property to the trustee; or, if the debtor refused to obey lawful orders of the court and failed to testify when required to do so. Complaint must be made before the later of one year after the granting of the discharge or the date the case is closed. The court, after notice and a hearing, may revoke the discharge on these grounds. 11 U.S.C. § 727(c), (d), & (e).

J. Special Tax Provisions

For purposes of state and local income taxes, the taxable period of a debtor that is an individual terminates on the date the order for relief is entered under chapter 7, unless the case was converted from chapter 11 or 12.

If an individual or corporate debtor has net taxable postpetition income, or if the debtor is a partnership, the trustee shall file a return for each taxable period during which the case was pending.

Special provision is made for the taxation of partnerships. 11 U.S.C. § 728.

VIII. CHAPTER 11 – REORGANIZATION

Most individuals or business that are eligible to file under chapter 7 may file for reorganization under chapter 11.[93] This chapter, however, is designed to accommodate complicated, publicly-held corporate reorganizations as well as those of lesser magnitude and, consequently, it is procedurally more elaborate and expensive to effectuate than a reorganization under chapter 12 or 13. To illustrate, this chapter contemplates the creation of creditor committees, the employment of professionals to assist the committees, the solicitation of creditor votes to accept or reject a reorganization plan, and the exchange and issuance of new securities by the debtor. The applicable time frames for action under chapter 11 are adjusted accordingly.

The Bankruptcy Reform Act of 1994 amended chapter 11 to expedite procedures for "small business" reorganizations.[94] A qualified small business debtor would be permitted to dispense with creditor committees; would have

---

[93] Although chapter 11 is clearly designed to facilitate business, i.e., corporate reorganization, an individual consumer debtor not engaged in business is permitted to file. Toibb v. Radloff, 111 S. Ct. 2197 (1991). The 1994 Reform Act amendments significantly raised the debt levels for filing under chapter 13. Hence, many individuals who could not file under chapter 13 and of necessity filed to reorganize under chapter 11, may now avail themselves of chapter 13.

[94] A "small business" is one defined as "a person engaged in commercial or business activities...whose aggregate noncontingent liquidated secured and unsecured debts as of the date of the petition do not exceed $2,000,000." 11 U.S.C. § 101(51C).

an exclusivity period for filing a plan of 100 days; and, would be subject to more liberal provisions for disclosure and solicitation of acceptances for a proposed reorganization plan.

Highlights of the statutory requirements for a chapter 11 reorganization are examined below.

A. Creditors' and Equity Security Holders' Committees

As soon as practicable after entry of an order for relief in a chapter 11 reorganization case, the U.S. Trustee appoints a committee of unsecured claim holders, and such additional committees as may be requested by a party or parties in interest. A small business debtor may, for cause, request the court to waive appointment of a creditors committee.

Ordinarily, the committee is composed of creditors willing to serve holding the seven largest claims of the kind represented by the committee (e.g., an equity security holders' committee would be composed of those persons holding the seven largest amounts of equity securities). Or, the committee might be comprised of the members of a creditor's committee organized before the order for relief if it was fairly chosen and is representative of the different kinds of claims to be represented.

If the committee membership is not representative of the different claims and interests, the court, on request of a party in interest, may order the appointment of additional committees. The U.S. Trustee will appoint the committees. 11 U.S.C. § 1102.

B. Power and Duties of Committees

A creditors' committee may:

- with court approval, employ accountants, attorneys, or other agents to represent or perform services for the committee;
- consult with the trustee or debtor in possession concerning the administration of the case;
- investigate the debtor's financial condition, the operation of its business and the desirability of continuing such business, and any other matter relevant to the case of the formulation of the plan;

- participate in the formulation of a plan and collect and file acceptance of the plan;
- request the appointment of a trustee or examiner if one has not been previously appointed; and
- perform such other services as are in the interest of those represented.

11 U.S.C. § 1103.

C. Appointment of Trustee or Examiner; Termination of the Trustee's Appointment

At any time after the commencement of the case but before confirmation of a plan, on request of a party in interest or the U.S. Trustee, the court, after notice and a hearing, may order the appointment of a trustee (1) for cause, including fraud, dishonesty, incompetence, or gross mismanagement of the affairs of the debtor by current management; or (2) if the appointment is in the interest of creditors.

If the court does not order the appointment of a trustee to run the debtor's business, it may appoint an examiner to conduct an investigation of the debtor, including an investigation of any allegations of fraud, dishonesty, incompetence, misconduct, mismanagement or irregularity, if the appointment is in the interests of creditors, or the debtor's unsecured debts to an insider exceed $5,000,000. 11 U.S.C. § 1104.

The court may, at any time before confirmation of a plan, terminate the trustee's appointment and restore the debtor to possession and management of the debtor's business. 11 U.S.C. § 1105.

D. Duties of a Trustee or Examiner

If a trustee or examiner is appointed in the manner discussed above, he or she must perform the following duties:

- account for all property received;
- if a purpose would be served, examine proofs of claims and object to improper claims;
- unless otherwise ordered by the court, furnish such information requested by a party in interest concerning the estate's administration;

- if operation of the debtor's business is authorized, file periodic reports and summaries of such operation, including a statement of receipts and disbursements, with those governmental units responsible for collecting and determining a tax:
- make and file a final report and account of the estate's administration with the court;
- if the debtor has not done so, file a list of creditors; a statement of the debtor's financial affairs; and a schedule of assets and liabilities;
- except to the extent the court orders otherwise, investigate the conduct and the financial condition of the debtor, the operation of the debtor's business and the desirability of the continuance of the business;
- file a statement with the court and with appropriate creditors' committee summarizing the investigation, including any facts pertaining to fraud, dishonesty, incompetence, misconduct, mismanagement, or irregularity in the management of the affairs of the debtor, or to a cause of action available to the estate;
- as soon as practicable, file a reorganization plan or a report of why the trustee will not file a plan, or recommend conversion of the case to one under chapter 7, 12, or 13, or dismissal;
- furnish information required by taxing authorities for any year for which the debtor has not filed a tax return; and
- after confirmation of a plan, file such reports as are necessary or as the court orders.

An examiner may be required to perform the investigative duties specified above, or any other duties of the trustee that the court orders the debtor in possession not to perform. 11 U.S.C. § 1106.

E. Rights, Powers, and Duties of a Debtor in Possession

This section places a debtor in possession in the shoes of a trustee in every way.[95] A debtor in possession has all the rights of a trustee with respect to management of the bankruptcy estate during reorganization, subject to such limitation or conditions as the court prescribes, and excluding the investigative and reporting duties which a trustee would perform. 11 U.S.C. § 1107.

---

[95] H.Rept. 95-595, supra note 16 at 404.

F. Authorization to Operate a Business

Unless the court orders otherwise, a chapter 11 debtor's business may continue to operate, i.e., it is not necessary to go to court to obtain an order authorizing the business' operation. 11 U.S.C. § 1108.

G. Right to be Heard

This provision grants the Securities and Exchange Commission the right to appear, raise, and be heard on any issue in a reorganization case, but not to appeal from any judgment, order, or decree entered in the case.

The same right to be heard is extended also to creditors, equity security holders, creditors' and equity security holders' committees, the debtor, the trustee, or any indenture trustee or other party in interest.[96] 11 U.S.C. § 1109.

H. Claims and Interests

In a chapter 11 reorganization, every unsecured creditor and equity security holder need not file a proof of claim. The debtor" schedules of claims will be accepted unless a claim is listed as disputed, contingent, or unliquidated.

A secured claim is treated as a recourse claim whether or not the claim is non-recourse. Thus, when a secured creditor is undersecured, the creditor will have an unsecured claim for the deficiency, regardless of whether a claim for the deficiency was permitted in the original loan. An additional benefit is conferred upon chapter 11 secured creditors which permits them to elect to be treated as secured up to the full amount of the allowable claim, even if it exceeds the value of the collateral. This preferred status terminates if the property securing the claim is sold during the proceeding or under the plan. The preferred status also terminates if the class (by at least 2/3rds in amount and more than 1/2 in number of the allowed claims) elects not to be

---

[96] Bankruptcy Rule 2018 gives the bankruptcy court discretion to permit any interested entity to intervene generally or with respect to any specified matter. It permits a State Attorney General to appear and be heard on behalf of consumer creditors if the court determines the appearance is in the public interest, but the Attorney General, like the SEC, may not appeal from a bankruptcy court decision. Likewise, in a chapter 9 or 11 case, a labor union or employees; association representative is given a right to be heard, but not a right of appeal.

so treated. A class may elect the application only if the security is not of inconsequential value and, if the creditor is a recourse creditor, the collateral is not sold during the proceeding or under the plan.

If the election is made, the claim is a secured claim to the extent that such claim is allowed (rather than, as provided elsewhere in the Code, a secured claim being secured only to the extent of the value of the collateral). 11 U.S.C. § 1111.

I. Rejection of Collective Bargaining Agreements

Prior to enactment of the Bankruptcy Amendments and Federal Judgeship Act of 1984, the Supreme Court held that collective bargaining agreements were executory contracts that could be rejected by a debtor.[97] In response to the Court's interpretation of a debtor's ability to reject a collective bargaining agreement in reorganization, Congress enacted a statute which prescribes the procedures that a trustee or a debtor in possession must take before it may alter the terms of or terminate a collective bargaining agreement.

After a petition is filed, if the debtor wishes to alter or terminate the collective bargaining agreement, it must supply the authorized representative of the employees complete and reliable information to demonstrate the need, in order to facilitate a reorganization, for the modifications to the employees' benefits and protections. The employee and debtor must engage in good faith negotiations with respect to proposals for alternation or termination of such agreements.

If the debtor files an application to reject a collective bargaining agreement, the court is directed to schedule a haring for not later than fourteen days after the filing. All interested parties may attend and participate in the hearing and the court should rule on the application within thirty days after the beginning of the hearing.

The court may approve the application for rejection only if it finds (i) that the debtor, prior tot he hearing, provided the authorized representative of the employees with the necessary information; (ii) the authorized representative has refused to accept the proposal without good cause; and, (iii) he balance of the equities clearly favors rejection.

---

[97] National Labor Relations Board v. Bildisco & Bildisco, 465 U.S. 513 (1984), holding that collective bargaining agreements are "executory contracts" under 11 U.S.C. 365 and may be rejected by a debtor unilaterally if the debtor can show that the agreement burdens the estate and that the equities balance in favor or rejection.

In addition the court may, after a hearing, authorize interim changes in the terms, conditions, wages, benefits or work rules provided by a collective bargaining agreement, when it is still in effect, if it is essential to the continuation of the debtor's business or is necessary to avoid irreparable damage to the estate. The implementation of interim changes does not, however, moot the procedures and requirements for an application for rejection. 11 U.S.C. § 1113.

J. Payment of Insurance Benefits to Retired Employees of the Debtor

Like § 1113 above, § 1114 of the Code deals with the treatment of a corporate debtor's employees, i.e., retirees, throughout the period of reorganization. Specifically, the debtor may not terminate retirees' health and life insurance benefits unless permitted to do so by the court, or with the consent of the retirees.[98]

The debtor must, subsequent to filing the bankruptcy petition and prior to filing an application to modify retiree benefits, negotiate with the authorized representatives of the retirees[99] and demonstrate the need for modifications in the retiree benefits based upon the most complete and reliable information available to permit the reorganization of the debtor and assure that all creditors, the debtor, and all affected parties will be treated fairly and equitably.

The court may enter an order providing for modification of retiree benefits if it finds that the debtor has fulfilled its disclosure and negotiation requirements, the authorized representative of the retirees has refused to accept the proposal without good cause, and, the modification is necessary to permit the reorganization of the debtor. The court may not enter a

---

[98] This provision, added to the Code in 1988 pursuant to P.L. 100-334, was enacted largely in response to the bankruptcy of the LTV Corporation. LTV, after filing a chapter 11 petition in 1986, immediately terminated the health and life insurance benefits of approximately 78,000 retirees. The retirees included those who received life and health insurance benefits pursuant to a collective bargaining agreement, and those who received benefits pursuant to non-collectively bargained plans. S.Rept. 119, 100th Congress, 1st Session 2 (1987).

[99] The law presumes that the authorized representative of retirees whose benefits are covered by a collective bargaining agreement will be the signatory labor organization unless it elects not to serve as authorized representative, or the court determines that different representation is appropriate. The court may appoint a committee of retired employees to act as authorized representative for employees whose benefits are not covered by a collective bargaining agreement, or for those whose are covered when the union declines to serve.

modification order which provides for benefits at a level lower than that proposed by the debtor. Nor does the entry of a modification order prohibit authorized representatives from applying to the court for an order increasing benefits at a later time.

When a modification order is filed, the court must schedule a hearing to be held not later than fourteen days after the filing of the application; it must rule on the application within ninety days after the commencement of the hearing. The court may, however, after notice and a haring, authorize interim modifications at any time prior to its issuing a final order if essential to the continuation of the debtor's business, or in order to avoid irreparable damage to the estate.

Payments of benefits to retirees prior to confirmation of a reorganization plan are to be treated as high priority administrative expenses. Such payments may not be deducted or offset from the amount allowed as claims for any benefits which remain unpaid, or from the amounts to be paid under the reorganization plan.

The limitations on the modifications of retiree benefits do not apply to any retiree, or the spouse of dependents of the retiree, if the retiree's gross income for the year preceding the bankruptcy filing exceeds $250,000 unless the retiree can demonstrate to the court that he is unable to obtain comparable health, medical, life, and disability coverage for himself, his spouse, and his dependents – who would otherwise be covered by the debtor's insurance plan.

K. The Reorganization Plan

1. Who May File A Plan

The debtor may file a plan with the petition in a voluntary case, or at any time in a voluntary or involuntary case.

After the order for relief is entered, the debtor has an exclusive 120 day period to file a plan. Any other party in interest, other than a U.S. Trustee, may file a plan if (i) a trustee has been appointed; (ii) the debtor has not filed a plan before 120 days after the order for relief; or, (iii) the debtor has not filed a plan that has been accepted by each class of impaired creditors (see *infra*) before 180 days after the entry of the order for relief. The court may extend the respective 120-day and 180-day periods "for cause."

A small business debtor has an exclusive 100 day period to file a plan. All plans must be filed within 160 days of the order for relief. On request of a party in interest, the court may, for cause, extend or reduce the time periods involved. But, the court may increase the debtor's 100-day period of exclusivity only if the debtor demonstrates the need for an increase "caused by circumstances for which the debtor should not be held accountable." 11 U.S.C. §§ 307, 1121.

2. Classification of Claims

The reorganization plan must place each claim or interest in a class that is substantially similar. An exception is provided in that the plan may designate a separate class of claims consisting only of every unsecured claim that is less than, or reduced to, an amount that the court approves as reasonable and necessary for administrative convenience, e.g., unsecured claims under $500. 11 U.S.C. § 1122.

3. Contents of the Plan

In order to be confirmed, the reorganization plan must meet specified statutory criteria. The plan must:

- designate classes of claims and interests as described above;
- specify any class of claims or interests that is not impaired under the plan;
- specify the treatment of impaired classes of claims and interests under the plan;
- provide the same treatment for each claim or interest of a particular class, unless the holder thereof agrees to a less favorable treatment of his claim or interest;
- provide adequate means for the plan's implementation, such as:
  i)   the debtor's retention of all or any part of the estate property;
  ii) the transfer of part or all of the estate property to one or more entities organized before or after the plans confirmation;
  iii) merger or consolidation of the debtor with one or more persons;
  iv) sale of all or any part of estate property either free of or subject to any lien, or the distribution thereof among those having an interest in such estate property;
  v)   satisfaction or modification of any lien;

vi) cancellation or modification of any indenture or similar instrument;

vii) curing or waiving and default;

viii) extending the maturity date, interest rate or other term of outstanding securities;

ix) amendment of the debtor's charter; or

x) issuance of securities of the debtor, or of any entity, for cash, property, existing securities, or in exchange for claims or interests, or for any other appropriate purpose;

- provide for inclusion in the corporate debtor's charter, or any corporate successor to the debtor, of a provision prohibiting the issuance of nonvoting equity securities and providing for an appropriate distribution of voting power. In the case of a class of equity securities having a dividend preference, the plan must have adequate provisions for the election of directors representing such a preferred class in the event of a default in the payment of such dividends; and

- contain only provisions that are consistent with the interest of creditors and equity security holders and with public policy with respect to the manner of selection of any officer, director, or trustee under the plan and any successor to such officer, director, or trustee.

Subject to the above conditions, the plan may:

- impair, or leave unimpaired, any class of claims, secured or unsecured, or of interests;

- subject to the Code provisions respecting executory contracts and unexpired leases, the plan must also provide for the assumption or rejection of any executory contract or unexpired lease not previously rejected pursuant to the Code;

- provide for the settlement of adjustment of any claim or interest belonging to the debtor or to the estate, or for the retention or enforcement of any claim or interest;

- provide for the sale of all or substantially all of the estate property with the distribution of the proceeds of sale among creditors and equity security holders;[100]

---

[100] Liquidations may be effected pursuant to a chapter 11 reorganization plan as well as under chapter 7's liquidation procedures. Hence, a debtor, e.g. a farmer, who is exempt from involuntary liquidation under chapter 7 of the Code but who voluntarily files under chapter

- modify the rights of holders of secured claims, other than a claim secured only by a security interest in real property that is the debtor's principal residence, or of holders of unsecured claims, or leave unaffected the rights of holders of any class of claims;[101] and
- any other provision that is not inconsistent with the Code.

In a case concerning an individual, a plan proposed by a party other than the debtor may not provide for the use, sale, or lease of the debtor's exempt property unless the debtor gives his consent.

If a plan proposes to cure a default, the amount necessary to cure it shall be determined in accordance with the underlying agreement and applicable nonbankruptcy law.[102] 11 U.S.C. § 1123.

4. Impairment of Claims or Interests

Simply put, an "impaired" claim is one that is materially and adversely affected by the bankruptcy and reorganization plan.[103] Impaired creditors have a greater role in the acceptance or rejection of a reorganization plan than those whose claims are relatively unaffected thereby. To be unimpaired, the treatment of a claim under the reorganization plan must satisfy one of three statutory criteria:

a. the plan must leave unaltered the legal, equitable, or contractual rights to which the claim or interest entitled its holder; or

b. the plan must cure the effect of a default that occurred before or after the commencement of a case, reinstate the maturity of such claim or interest, compensate the holder for damages incurred as a result of the reinstatement, and, leave unaltered the legal, equitable,

---

11 may ultimately be subject to another party in interest's proposal for a reorganization plan that is essentially a liquidation plan.

[101] This provision, added to the Code by § 206 of the 1994 Reform Act, is intended to conform the treatment of residential mortgages in chapter 11 to that of chapter 13, preventing bifurcation and lien stripping of home mortgages. See, 11 U.S.C. § 1322(b)(2), discussed infra.

[102] This provision, added by § 304 of the 1994 Reform Act, is intended to overrule the U.S. Supreme Court decision in Rake v. Wade, 113 S. Ct. 2187 (1993) which held that the Code required interest to be paid by debtors curing mortgage arrearages notwithstanding the underlying agreement or state law. This amendment operates prospectively only, however, to agreements entered after the date of enactment, October 22, 1994.

[103] See S. Rept. 95-989, supra note 16 at 20.

or contractual rights to which the claim or interest entitles the holder.[104]

11 U.S.C. § 1124.

5. Postpetition Disclosure and Solicitation

In order to have a reorganization plan accepted, the debtor, other than a small business debtor, must provide creditors with information about the proposed plan and solicit votes accepting it. Although the debtor may not solicit votes accepting the plan without prior court approval, the debtor may negotiate with various creditors and creditor committees throughout the period in which the plan is formulated.

The Code prohibits solicitation of votes accepting or rejecting a plan after the filing of a case unless, at the time of or before such solicitation, there is transmitted to the solicitee (creditor) either the plan or a summary of the plan, and a written disclosure statement approved by the court as containing adequate information.

A small business debtor may solicit acceptances based on a disclosure statement that is conditionally approved by the bankruptcy court and mailed to creditors at least 10 days prior to the confirmation hearing so long as the debtor provides adequate information to creditors.

"Adequate information" is defined to mean information in sufficient detail to enable a hypothetical reasonable investor to make an informed judgment about the plan, but need not include information about any other possible or proposed plans.

Although a court may approve a disclosure statement without a valuation of the debtor or his assets, in some cases a valuation and appraisal may be necessary to develop adequate information.

The bankruptcy court's decision whether a disclosure statement contains adequate information is not governed by any otherwise applicable nonbankruptcy law, rule, or regulation. However, the official or agency responsible for administering or enforcing such law, rule, or regulation, e.g., the Securities and Exchange Commission or a State Corporation Commission, may appear and be heard on the issue, but may not appeal an order approving a disclosure statement. Likewise, an individual who solicits acceptance or rejection of a plan, in good faith and in compliance with the

---

[104] Amendments to this provision effected by § 213 of the Bankruptcy Reform Act of 1994 were designed to overrule case law holding that unsecured creditors are denied the right to receive postpetition interest on their allowed claims even though a debtor is liquidation and reorganization solvent. H. Rept. 103-835 at 47-48.

applicable provisions of the Code, or who participates in the offer, issuance, sale or purchase of a security offered or sold under the plan, is not liable on account of such activities for violation of securities laws that are rendered nonapplicable in the bankruptcy forum. 11 U.S.C. § 1125.

6. Acceptance of the Plan

Claim and interest holders, or, in the case of the United States, the Secretary of the Treasure, are permitted to accept or reject a plan of reorganization. With respect to prepetition solicitation, an acceptance or rejection is valid so long as the solicitation was in compliance with applicable nonbankruptcy laws governing disclosure, or it is occurred after disclosure of "adequate information" in compliance with the Code.

The Code makes certain presumptions with respect to postpetition solicitation and acceptance. A class of claims or interests is deemed to accept a plan if it is not impaired thereunder. In this case, solicitation is not required. Contrarily, if the reorganization plan provides that the claims or interests of a certain class do not entitle its holders to any payment or compensation, they are deemed to reject the plan.

Of the classes of claim holders who actually vote, a class has accepted a plan when creditors (excluding any whose acceptance or rejection was not in good faith) holding two-thirds in amount and more than one-half in number of the allowed claims cast votes in favor therefor. A class of interests has accepted a plan if it has been accepted, in good faith, by holders of two-thirds in amount of the allowed interest of such class. 11 U.S.C. § 1126.

7. Modification of the Plan

The proponent of a plan may modify it at any time before confirmation. After confirmation and before substantial consummation, it may be modified at any time by the plan's proponent or the reorganized debtor.

The modified plan must be in compliance with chapter 11's provisions regarding classification of claims and interests; contents of a plan; and post-petition disclosure and solicitation.

The pre-confirmation modified plan becomes the plan when it is filed with the court. The post-confirmation modifications take place only if the court, after notice and hearing, confirms the plan as modified. Any holder of a claim or interest that has accepted or rejected the plan is deemed to have accepted or rejected, as the case may be, the plan as modified unless, within the time fixed by the court, such holder changes the previous acceptance or rejection. 11 U.S.C. § 1127.

L. Confirmation of a Reorganization Plan

1. Confirmation Hearing
After notice, the court holds a confirmation hearing at which a party in interest may appear and enter any objections to the plan's confirmation by the court. 11 U.S.C. § 1128.

2. Confirmation of the Plan
In order for the court to confirm a reorganization plan, it must satisfy all of the statutory requirements:

1. the plan, and its proponent, have complied with the applicable provisions of the chapter;

2. the plan was proposed in good faith and not by any means forbidden by law;

3. payments made, or promised, for services, costs, or expenses, either in or incident to, or in connection with a case or plan, must (i) be disclosed to the court, (ii) be reasonable, or (iii) be approved as reasonable by the court if such payment is to be fixed after confirmation;

4. the plan's proponent has disclosed the identity and affiliation of any individual proposed to serve as an officer of the reorganized debtor after confirmation, and the appointment is consistent with the interests of the creditors, equity security holders, and public policy; and, the proponent has disclosed the identify of any insider that will be employed or retained by the reorganized debtor, and the nature of any compensation for such insider;

5. any regulatory commission having jurisdiction over the debtor after confirmation of the plan has approved any rate change provided for in the plan, or, in the alternative, such rate change is expressly conditioned on such approval;

6. with respect to each class of impaired claims or interests, (i) each holder of claim or interest has accepted the plan, or will receive under the plan property of a value that is not less than the amount that the holder would receive if the debtor were liquidated under

chapter 7;[105] or (ii) if a class of undersecured creditors has elected to be treated as a secured creditor to the extent of the value of the collateral securing their claim, and as an unsecured creditor for the amount of the deficiency between their debt and such value, each claimholder of the class will receive or retain, on account of such claim, property of a value that is not less than the value of such creditor's interest in the estate's interest in the property securing the claim;

7. with respect to each class, such class has accepted the plan or is not impaired under the plan;

8. except to the extent that a holder of a particular claim has agreed to a different treatment of such claim, the plan provides that each holder:

   (A) of an administrative expense claim and an "involuntary gap" claim will receive cash equal to the allowed amount of such claim;

   (B) in a class of claims for (i) wages, salaries, commissions, vacation, severance and sick leave pay; (ii) contributions to employee benefit plans; and, (iii) deposits in connection with the purchase, lease, or rental of property, each claimholder of a claim of such class will receive cash equal to the allowed amount of such claim if the class has not accepted the plan;

9. at least one class of claims has accepted the plan, determined without including any acceptance of the plan by an "insider" holding a claim of such class;

10. confirmation of the plan is not likely to be followed by the liquidation, or the need for further financial reorganization of the debtor, or any successor to the debtor under the plan unless such liquidation or reorganization is proposed in the plan;

11. all bankruptcy fees have been paid, or will be paid under the plan.

The Code does permit the court, in specified circumstances, to confirm a reorganization plan when one or more classes of impaired creditors have voted not to accept it. The court may do so when it finds that "the plan does

---

[105] The requirement that creditors under a reorganization plan receive as much or more than they would receive if the debtor were liquidated under chapter 7 is known as "the best interests of the creditor" test. It is an important yardstick for measuring the viability of a reorganization plan.

not discriminate unfairly, and is fair and equitable, with respect to each class of claims or interests that is impaired under, and has not accepted the plan."[106] In order for a plan to meet the statutory criteria of "fair and equitable," it must satisfy the following requirements:

1. Secured creditors must retain the lien and receive on account of the claim deferred cash payments equal to the value of the allowed claim as of the effective date of the plan; or, if the property securing the claim is sold, the lien must attach to the proceeds; or, the creditors must receive the "indubitable equivalent" of the claim;

2. Unsecured creditors must receive property of a value as of the effective date of the plan equal to the allowed amount of such claim; or, no junior claim or interest holder will receive anything;

3. Each class of interests must receive or retain property of a value equal to the greater of (i) the allowed amount of any fixed liquidation preference to which such holder is entitled; (ii) any fixed redemption price to which such holder is entitled; or (iii) in the absence of such value, then no junior interest holder will receive anything.[107]

The court may confirm only one reorganization plan, unless a confirmation order has been revoked. If confirmation requirements are met by more than one submitted plan, the court must consider the preferences of creditors and equity security holders in determining which plan to confirm. The court may not confirm a plan if its principal purpose if the avoidance of

---

[106] The authority of the court to approve a reorganization plan over the dissent of impaired creditors is referred to as "cramdown" authority.

[107] The principle that a dissenting class of unsecured creditors must be provided for in full before any junior class can receive or retain any property under the plan is known as "the absolute priority rule." It is codified at 11 U.S.C. § 1129(b)(2)(B)&(C). The rule had its genesis in judicial construction of the undefined requirement under bankruptcy law prior to the Code the reorganization plans be "fair and equitable." See, Northern Pacific R. Co. v. Boyd, 228 U.S. 482 (1913).

The Court interpreted the rule to prohibit a debtor farmer from retaining equity in farm property under a reorganization plan where senior classes of unsecured creditors were to receive less than the full amount of their claim and where the debtor's contribution of new value consisted of a promise of future performance. Norwest Bank Worthington v. Ahlers, 485 U.S. 197 (1988).

In a typical corporate reorganization, the plan would provide for payment to administrative and other priority claimants, secured claimants, unsecured claimants, and stockholders. Under the absolute priority rule, if classes of unsecured creditors reject the plan, they must receive the full amount of their allowed claims before stockholders may realize any distribution.

taxes or the avoidance of specified provisions under federal securities law.11 U.S.C. § 1129.

3. Effect of Confirmation

The provisions of a confirmed plan bind the debtor and any entity issuing securities or acquiring property under the plan; it binds all impaired, unimpaired, accepting and unaccepting creditors, equity security holders, and general partners. Except as otherwise provided in the plan, confirmation vests all of the property of the estate in the debtor, and the property dealt with by the plan is free and clear of all claims and interests of creditors, equity security holders, and of general partners.

Except as otherwise provided, confirmation discharges the debtor from all debts in existence when the case was filed, debts which arose after the filing and before the order of confirmation, all debts arising from the rejection of executory contracts and unexpired leases, claims arising from the recovery of property, and specified post-petition debts with priority status owing to taxing authorities.

Confirmation does not discharge an individual debtor from any debt excepted from discharge under § 523 of the Code. Nor does it discharge a debtor if the plan provides for the liquidation of all or substantially all of the property of the estate; if the debtor does not engage in business after consummation of the plan; and, if the debtor would be denied a discharge under chapter 7 if the case were a case under chapter 7. 11 U.S.C. § 1141.

4. Revocation of an Order of Confirmation

On request of a party in interest at any time before 180 days after the entry date of the confirmation order, the court, after notice and hearing, may revoke such order if and only if it was procured by fraud.

A court order revoking the confirmation must revoke the discharge of the debtor and contain any provision necessary to protect any entity acquiring rights in good faith reliance on the confirmation. 11 U.S.C. § 1144.

M. Implementation of the Plan

Notwithstanding any otherwise applicable nonbankruptcy law, rule, or regulation relating to financial condition, the debtor and any entity organized to carry out the plan shall do so and comply with any order of the court.

The court may direct the debtor, and any other necessary party, to execute or deliver any instrument required to effect a transfer of property dealt with by a confirmed plan, and to perform any other act, including the satisfaction of any lien, that is necessary for the consummation of the plan. 11 U.S.C. § 1142.

N. Participation in Distribution

The Code fixes a five year limitation (running from the date of entry of the order of confirmation) for presentment or surrender of securities or the performance of any other act that is a condition to participation in distribution under the plan. Failure to take the appropriate action bars the entity from participation in the distribution under the plan. 11 U.S.C. § 1143.

O. Exemption from Securities Laws

The Code grants limited exemptions from the registration and prospectus requirements of § 5 of the Securities and Exchange Act of 1933, 15 U.S. C. § 77e, and state and local registration requirements respecting the offer of sale of a security and the registration or licensing of an issuer or underwriter of, or a broker or dealer in, securities.

The limited exemption applies to:

- the offer or sale, under the plan, of securities in exchange for a claim (including an administrative expense claim) against, or an interest in, the case of the debtor, an affiliate in a joint case, or a successor;
- the offer or sale of a security through, or upon the exercise of, any warrant, option, subscription right, or conversion privilege;
- offers and sales of a limited amount of unregistered portfolio securities owned by the debtor;
- creditors and equity interest holders who receive a security pursuant to the plan if they resell the security within 40 days of the public offering by the issuer or underwriter, provided a disclosure statement approved under the Code has been provided at or before the time of such transaction by such stockholder.

The Code also provides that an offer of sale of securities under the plan is deemed a public offering; and, that the Trust Indenture Act of 1939, 15 U.S. C. § 77aaa *et seq.*, does not apply to a commercial note issued under the plan and maturing not later than one year after the plan's effective date.[108] 11 U.S.C. § 1145.

P. Special Tax Provisions

For state and local income tax purposes, the taxable period of a debtor that is an individual terminates on the date of the order for relief under chapter 11 unless the case was converted from chapter 7.

The trustee must file state or local income tax returns for the estate of an individual debtor under chapter 11 for each taxable period after the order for relief during which the case is pending.

The issuance, transfer, or exchange of a security of a confirmed plan may not be taxed under any law imposing a stamp tax or similar tax.[109]

The court may authorize the proponent of a reorganization plan to request a determination from a state or local income tax authority of questions of law regarding the tax effect of the plan. In the event of an actual controversy, the court may declare such effects after either the response of the governmental unit or 270 days after the request is made. 11 U.S.C. § 1146.

IX. CHAPTER 13 – ADJUSTMENTS OF DEBTS OF AN INDIVIDUAL WITH REGULAR INCOME

Chapter 13 contemplates a more expedited and streamlined procedure for individual, i.e., consumer reorganization than that provided for under chapter 11. In contrast to chapter 11, a chapter 13 reorganization always requires the participation of a standing trustee. It does not establish creditor committees, nor do creditors vote to accept or reject a plan of reorganization, although they are given the opportunity to accept certain provisions and

---

[108] The Trust Indenture Act sets registration and prospectus requirements for indentures (mortgages, deeds of trust, trust, and other indenture or similar agreements) under which there has been, or is to be, issued a security in respect of which a particular registration statement has been filed.

[109] Certain real estate transfer taxes may be preempted as well if they share the characteristics of a "stamp tax." See In re Jacoby-Bender, Inc. 34 B.R. 60 (Bankr.E.D.N.Y. 1983).

interpose objections. Only the debtor may propose the reorganization plan, which must be completed within a specified three to five year time frame. A debtor receives a discharge of indebtedness not upon confirmation, but upon completion of all payments under the plan. The more significant procedural features are examined below.

A. Stay of Action against Codebtor

In addition to the automatic stay, which operates to prevent creditors from engaging in collection activities after an order for relief is filed, chapter 13 imposes an additional stay on creditor attempts to collect on consumer debts[110] against those who may be liable with the debtor. The purpose of this provision is to protect a chapter 13 debtor by insulating him from indirect pressures from his creditors exerted through friends or relatives that may have cosigned an obligation of the debtor and who otherwise may be subject to the creditor's collection efforts.[111]

Specifically, a creditor may not act, commence, or continue any civil action to collect a consumer debt from any individual that is liable on the debt with the debtor, or that secured such debt unless (1) the individual became liable on the debt in the ordinary course of the individual's business, or (2) the case is closed, dismissed, or converted to a case under chapters 7 or 11.

A creditor may, however, present a negotiable instrument and give notice of dishonor to preserve his rights under applicable nonbankruptcy law.

Likewise, a party in interest may ask the court for relief from the stay on the grounds that:

- as between the debtor and the nonbankrupt codebtor, the codebtor received the consideration for the claim held by the creditor;
- the plan filed by the debtor proposes not to pay such claim; or
- the creditor's interest would be irreparably harmed by continuation of such stay.

---

[110] "Consumer debts" are debts incurred by an individual primarily for a personal, family, or household purpose. 11 U.S.C. § 101(8).

[111] H.Rept. 95-595, supra note 16 at 426.

If the court has not ruled on the request for relief from the stay within twenty days of the creditor's request therefor, the stay will be terminated unless the debtor or the codebtor files a written objection thereto. 11 U.S.C. § 1301.

B. The Trustee

1. Appointment

The U.S. Trustee may appoint a standing trustee from a panel of eligible, private trustees. Otherwise, the U.S. Trustee may appoint a disinterested individual to serve, or the U.S. Trustee may serve. 11 U.S.C. § 1302(a); 28 U.S.C. § 586.

2. Duties of the Trustee

Among the duties which the trustee, as principal administrator in the case, must perform are:

- be accountable for all property received;
- make sure the debtor files a statement of intent with respect to the retention or surrender of certain consumer goods;
- investigate the debtor's financial affairs;
- if a purpose would be served, examine proofs of claims and object to the allowance of improper claims;
- if advisable, oppose the debtor's discharge;
- unless otherwise ordered by the court, furnish such information as may be requested by a party in interest concerning the estate and its administration;
- make, and file with the court, a final report and account of the administration;
- appear and be heard at any hearing that concerns (i) the value of property subject to a lien, (ii) confirmation of a plan, or (iii) modification of a plan after confirmation;
- advise, other than on legal matters, and assist the debtor in the performance of the plan;
- ensure that the debtor commences making timely payments under the plan;

- if the debtor is in business, investigate the financial condition of the debtor, the operation of the debtor's business, and the desirability of continuing the business, and report such information to the court.

11 U.S.C. § 1302.

C. Rights and Powers of the Debtor

A debtor may sell, use, or lease estate property:

- other than in the ordinary course of business, after notice and hearing;
- in the ordinary course of business without a hearing so long as such use is not inconsistent with conditions imposed or relief granted under the automatic stay, and so long as the creditor's interest in the property is adequately protected;
- the debtor may sell property free and clear of any creditor's interest in the property only if applicable nonbankruptcy law permits sale of such property, the creditor consents, the price at which the property is to be sold is greater than the aggregate value of all liens on the property, the interest is in a bona fide dispute or the creditor could be compelled to accept a money satisfaction of the interest;
- notwithstanding any provision of a contract, a leas, or applicable law that is conditioned on the insolvency of financial condition of the debtor, or on the commencement of a case in bankruptcy.

11 U.S.C. § 1303.

D. Debtor Engaged in Business

The Code stipulates that a self-employed debtor who incurs trade credit in the production of income from such employment is engaged in business. Because chapter 13 is limited to individuals, any business being operated can only be a sole proprietorship if the debts of the business are to be dealt with under chapter 13.

Unless the court orders otherwise, a debtor engaged in business may operate the business and use, sale or lease property of the estate in the ordinary course of business without notice and hearing. The debtor may not use, sell or lease cash collateral (i.e., cash, negotiable instruments, documents of title, securities, deposit accounts, etc.) unless the entity having an interest in the collateral consents or the court, after notice and hearing, authorizes the use.

The debtor may obtain unsecured credit and incur unsecured debt as an administrative expense in the ordinary course of business; he may obtain trade credit and incur trade debt with some special priority or superpriority if necessary if the court, after notice and hearing, authorizes it.

In addition, a debtor operating a business must file periodic reports and summaries of its operation, including a statement of receipts and disbursements, with any governmental unit charged with the responsibility for determining and collecting any tax arising out of such operation. 11 U.S.C. § 1304.

E. Filing and Allowance of Postpetition Claims

This provision is applicable exclusively to chapter 13 and supplements other provisions of the Code, 11 U.S.C. §§ 501-510, which deal with the filing and allowance of claims. It permits the filing of a proof of claim for taxes that become payable while the case is pending; or, for a consumer debt that arises after the order for relief, and that is for property or services necessary for the debtor's performance.

The allowance of such claims is governed by § 502, except that its standards are applied as of the date of the claim" allowance rather than as of the date of the filing of the petition.

A postpetition consumer debt claim that is for property or services necessary for the debtor's performance under the plan will be disallowed if the claimholder knew or should have known that the trustee's prior approval for the debtor's incurring of the obligation was practicable and was not obtained. 11 U.S.C. § 1305.

F. Property of the Estate

In addition to the other Code provisions delineating what constitutes property of the bankruptcy estate,[112] chapter 13 includes earnings from all services performed by the debtor after the commencement of the case but

---

[112] 11 U.S.C. § 541. See discussion supra.

before the case is closed, dismissed, or converted to one under chapter 7 or 11.

A chapter 13 debtor is permitted to remain in possession of all property of the estate despite Code provision elsewhere[113] requiring a debtor to surrender to a trustee all property of the estate, including books, documents, records, and papers relating to property of the estate. 11 U.S.C. § 1306.

G. The Reorganization Plan

1. Filing

Only the debtor may file a chapter 13 reorganization plan. 11 U.S.C. § 1321. The Code specifies no time period for filing, but Bankruptcy Rule 3015 provides that if a plan is not filed with the petition, it must be filed within 15 days thereafter.

2. Contents of the Plan

A chapter 13 reorganization plan must:

- provide for the submission of all or such portion of future earnings of the debtor to the supervision and control of the trustee as is necessary for the execution of the plan;
- provide for the full payment, in deferred cash payments, of all claims entitled to priority under the Code, 11 U.S.C. § 507, unless the holder of a particular claim agrees to a different treatment of such claim; and
- if the plan classifies claims, provide the same treatment for each claim within a particular class.

The plan may:
- divide unsecured claims which are not entitled to priority into classes, provided that no class is discriminated against unfairly. The plan may, however, treat claims for a consumer debt of the debtor for which a third-party is liable with the debtor differently than other unsecured claims;

---

[113] 11 U.S.C. § 521(4).

- modify the rights of secured and unsecured claimholders,[114] other than a claim secured only by a security interest (i.e., a lien created by agreement, such as a mortgage) in real property that is the debtor's principal residence;[115]
- provide for the curing or waiving of any default;
- provide for concurrent payments on secured and unsecured claims;
- cure any default on any secured or unsecured claim on which the final payment under the plan is due;
- provide for payment of all or any part of a postpetition claim;
- provide for the assumption or rejection of executory contracts and unexpired leases;
- provide for payment of all or any part of a claim from the debtor's property or estate property;
- on confirmation of the plan, or at a later time, provide for the vesting of estate property in the debtor or any other entity; and
- include any other provision not inconsistent with the Code.

The plan may not provide for payments over a period that is longer than three years, unless the court, for cause, approves a longer period, but the court may not approve a period that is longer than five years.

A debtor may cure a default with respect to a lien upon the debtor's principal residence until such time as the residence is sold at foreclosure; when a final payment is due under a home mortgage *before* the date on which the final payment under the plan is due, the plan may provide for the claim as modified for the duration of the reorganization plan.[116]

---

[114] A debtor was permitted to include a mortgage lien on farm property in a chapter 13 plan even after the debtor's personal liability on the debt secured by the property has been discharged in a chapter 7 liquidation. Johnson v. Home State Bank, 111 S. Ct. 2150 (1991).

[115] Despite Code language prohibiting the "modification: of a home mortgage, several lower courts permitted debtors to bifurcate a home mortgage into a secured and unsecured claim. In Nobelman v. American Saving Bank, 113 S. Ct. 2106 (1993), the Supreme Court held unanimously that a chapter 13 debtor may not "strip down" a mortgage on the debtor's principal residence, i.e., reduce an undersecured claim to its fair market value.

[116] These provisions, strengthening a debtor's ability to rescue a home under chapter 13, were enacted pursuant to § 301 of the Bankruptcy Reform Act of 1994. Even though a debtor may not modify the amount of a home mortgage lien, these provisions, overturning case law to the contrary, permit the debtor to cure defaults up to the time of foreclosure under state law, and allow the debtor to spread payments over the duration of the reorganization plan even if a final payment was due prior thereto.

If a plan proposes to cure a default, the amount necessary to cure it shall be determined in accordance with the underlying agreement and applicable nonbankruptcy law.[117] 11 U.S.C. § 1322.

3. Payments under the Plan

Unless the court orders otherwise, the debtor must begin making payments proposed by a plan within 30 days after the plan is filed.

Payments are retained by the trustee until confirmation or denial of confirmation. If the plan is confirmed, the trustee will distribute payments in accordance with the plan as soon as practicable. If the plan is not confirmed, the trustee will return payments to the debtor after deducting administrative expenses.

Before or at the time of each payment to creditors under the plan, the trustee will pay outstanding administrative expenses and trustee fees. Except as otherwise provided in the plan or the confirmation order, the trustee will make the payments to the creditors under the plan. 11 U.S.C. § 1326.

4. Modification of the Plan before Confirmation

The debtor may modify the plan at any time before confirmation, so long as the modifications are consistent with Code requirements.

After the debtor files the modifications, the plan as modified becomes the plan.

Any holder of a secured claim that has accepted or rejected the plan is deemed to have accepted or rejected, as the case may be, the plan as modified, unless the modification provides for a change in the rights of the holder, in which case the holder may change his previous acceptance or rejection. 11 U.S.C. § 1323.

---

[117] this provision, added by § 304 of the Bankruptcy Reform Act of 1994, is intended to overrule the U.S. Supreme Court decision in Rake v. Wade, 113 S. Ct. 2187 (1993) which held that the Code required interest to be paid by debtors curing mortgage arrearages notwithstanding the underlying agreement or state law. This amendment operates prospectively only, however, to agreements entered after the date of enactment, October 22, 1994.

H. Confirmation

1. Confirmation Hearing

After notice, the court will hold a hearing on confirmation of the plan during which any party in interest may interpose an objection.

2. Confirmation of the Plan

The court shall confirm a plan if it meets the following criteria:

- it complies with all applicable Code provisions;
- the required filing fees and court costs have been paid;
- the plan was proposed in good faith and is not in any way forbidden by law;
- the value of the property to be distributed under the plan on account of each allowed unsecured claim is not less than the amount that would be paid if the debtor's estate were liquidated under chapter 7;
- with respect to each allowed secured claim provided for by the plan, the holder has accepted the plan, or the plan provides that the claimholder retain the lien securing the claim and the value of the property to be distributed on account of such claim is not less than the allowed amount of such claim, or the debtor surrenders the property securing the claim to the holder;[118]
- the debtor will be able to comply with, and make all payments under the plan.

If the trustee or a holder of an allowed unsecured claim objects to the confirmation, the court may not approve it unless (a) the value of the property to be distributed under the plan on account of such claim is not less than the amount of such claim, or (b) the plan provides that all of the

---

[118] In Associates Commercial Corp. v. Rash, 117 S. Ct. 1879 (1997), the Court resolved a dispute regarding the proper valuation of property when a debtor exercises the "cram down" option. Specifically, the Court determined that when a debtor, over a secure creditor" objection, seeks to retain and use the creditor" collateral, the value of the collateral should, pursuant to 11 U.S.C. § 506(a) be a replacement-value standard. The Court reached that conclusion after considering whether the value of the collateral should be determined by (1) what the secured creditor could obtain through foreclosure sale of the property (the "foreclosure-value" standard); (2) what the debtor would have to pay for comparable property (the "replacement-value" standard); or, (3) the midpoint between these two measurements.

debtor's projected disposable income to be received during the three-year period will be applied to make payments under the plan.

"Disposable income" means income which is not reasonably necessary for the maintenance and support of the debtor and his or her dependents and for the payment of necessary business expenses if the debtor is in business. Necessary maintenance and support includes charitable contributions of up to 15 percent of the debtor's gross annual income.

After the confirmation of a plan, the court may order any entity from whom the debtor receives income to pay all or any part of such income to the trustee. 11 U.S.C. § 1325.

3. Effect of Confirmation

The provisions of a confirmed plan bind the debtor and each creditor, whether or not the claim of the creditor is provided for by the plan or whether or not the creditor has accepted or rejected the plan.

Except as otherwise provided in the plan or the order confirming it, confirmation vests all estate property in the debtor free and clear of any creditor's claim or interest provided for by the plan. 11 U.S.C. § 1328.

4. Modification of Plan after Confirmation

At any time prior to completion of payments under the confirmed plan, the plan may be modified upon the request of the debtor, the trustee, or the holder of an allowed unsecured claim to:

- increase or reduce payments to creditors of a particular class;
- extend or reduce the time for such payments; or
- alter the payment to a creditor to take account of payment of his claim from sources other than under the plan.

The previously delineated requirements relating to the contents and confirmation of a plan, as well as those relating to a creditor's acceptance or rejection of a pre-confirmation modification of a plan, apply to a post-confirmation modification. Additionally, the modification must take place within the original three-year time period, with extensions to no longer than five years. 11 U.S.C. § 1329.

5. Revocation of a Confirmation Order

On request of a party in interest and after notice and hearing, the court may revoke a confirmation order at any time within 180 days after its entry, if the confirmation was procured by fraud. Thereafter, unless a modified plan is confirmed, the court must either dismiss the case or convert it to a chapter 7 or chapter 11 case. 11 U.S.C. § 1330.

I. Discharge

1. Time and Scope of Discharge

As soon as practicable after the debtor's completion of payments under the plan, unless the court approves a written waiver of discharge executed by the debtor, the court shall grant the debtor a discharge of all debts provided for by the plan or disallowed by the court.

Although narrowed significantly by amendments to the Code in 1990, a chapter 13 discharge remains potentially of broader scope than one under chapters 7, 11, or 12. Debts which are nondischargeable under chapter 13 are: those for any unsecured or secured claim on which the last payment is due after the date on which the final payment under the plan is due; for debts to a spouse, former spouse, or child of the debtor, for alimony, maintenance and support; for liability for death or injury caused by the debtor while driving while intoxicated;[119] for criminal restitution;[120] criminal fines;[121] and, for student loans.[122] There is no prohibition against a plan provision for partial or no payment of a debt based on fraud, fiduciary defalcation, embezzlement or larceny, willful or malicious injury to person or property, a governmental fine or penalty (excluding criminal restitution obligations) –

---

[119] Two legislative enactments having virtually identical language entitled the Criminal Victims protection Act of 1990 amend chapter 13 to make DWI judgments nondischargeable: P.L. 101-581 (Nov. 14, 1990), and P.L. 101-647, Title XXXI, §§ 3102(b) and 3103 (Nov. 29, 1990).

[120] In Kelly v. Robinson, supra, the U.S. Supreme Court interpreted language creating exceptions to discharge under chapter 7 and held that restitution obligations imposed as conditions of probation in state criminal actions were nondischargeable. In 1990, in Pennsylvania v. Davenport, 110 S. Ct. 2126, the Court held that those obligations were dischargeable under chapter 13. The Criminal Victims protection Acts, P.L. 101-581, P.L. 101-647, amended the Code to provide that criminal restitution obligations are nondischargeable under chapter 13.

[121] This exception to dischargeability was added by § 302 of the Bankruptcy Reform Act of 1994.

[122] P.L. 101-508, §§ 3007, 3008. Nondischargeability for student loans under chapter 13 was originally legislated to sunset on October 1, 1996. The sunset provision was repealed by P.L. 102-325, § 1558, 106 Stat. 841 (July 23, 1992).

all of which are nondischargeable under chapters 7, 11, and 13 pursuant to 11 U.S.C. § 523. 11 U.S.C. § 1328(a).

2. Hardship Discharge

Despite the fact that a debtor does not complete all the payments provided for under the plan, the court may grant the debtor a discharge if:

- the debtor's failure to complete payments is due to circumstances for which he should not justly be held accountable;
- the value of the property actually distributed under the plan on account of each allowed unsecured claim is not less than the amount that would have been paid on the claim if the debtor's estate had been liquidated under chapter 7; and
- modification of the plan is impracticable.

11 U.S.C. § 1328(b).

3. Effect of a Hardship Discharge

A hardship discharge relieves the debtor from all unsecured debts provided for by the plan or disallowed by the court, but reinstates the nondischargeability of debts under § 523(a). Long term secured and unsecured debts which were not due until after the date on which final payment would have been due under the plan are also nondischargeable. Hence, the "superdischarge" which might otherwise be available under chapter 13 is unavailable in connection with the nonperforming hardship discharge. 11 U.S.C. § 1328(c).

4. Effect of Discharge on a Postpetition Consumer Debt

A postpetition consumer debt is not discharged if prior trustee approval of the incurring of the debt was practicable and was not obtained. 11 U.S.C. § 1328(d).

5. Revocation of Discharge

At the request of any party in interest within one year after the discharge was granted, the court, after notice and haring, may revoke the discharge if it was obtained through fraud and the requesting party learned of the fraud after the discharge was granted. 11 U.S.C. § 1328(e).

CHAPTER 11 BANKRUPTCY: THE ECONOMIC ISSUES

Mark Jickling

Chapter 11 bankruptcy is designed not just to provide for an equitable distribution of a bankrupt firm's assets among its creditors, but it offers distressed firms an alternative to liquidation, a chance to reorganize and continue as going concerns. The premise of Chapter 11 is that economic assets are more valuable employed for the purpose for which they were assembled than if they are sold piecemeal. Thus, liquidation of firms as soon as they are unable to pay their bills can be destructive of economic value. In adopting the Chapter 11 procedure in 1978, Congress hoped to save jobs and enhance economic efficiency.

The Bankruptcy Reform Act of 1994 (P.L. 103-394) created a National Bankruptcy Review Commission, whose mission is to examine the bankruptcy code from top to bottom and report to Congress by October 20, 1997, with recommendations for reform. Chapter 11 will likely be high on the Commission's agenda, since it has been under attack for a number of years. Critics have argued that the procedure is saddled with a variety of costs that could be lowered by streamlining the reorganization process, by replacing it with an alternative mechanism, or by simple abolition. This report surveys the economic issues that underlie the debate over Chapter 11 and looks at research into the costs and benefits of Chapter 11 and some of the proposed alternatives.

HOW CHAPTER 11 WORKS

The Legal Procedure

Chapter 11 is a product of the Bankruptcy Reform Act of 1978 (P.L. 98-598), which replaced the existing bankruptcy law in its entirety. Chapter 11 provides for the reorganization, rather than the liquidation, of financially troubled firms. When a Chapter 11 petition is filed,[1] the company continues to operate under the supervision of the bankruptcy court. The court has the option of appointing a bankruptcy trustee to run the firm's operations, but in most cases (unless the court finds fraud, dishonesty, incompetence, or gross mismanagement) the existing management remains in control and becomes known, in bankruptcy parlance, as the "debtor in possession." As in all bankruptcy proceedings, once the Chapter 11 petition is filed, the "automatic stay" goes into effect; that is, all debt payments are suspended and individual creditors may not seek to collect what is due them. Instead, the bankruptcy court groups the creditors and shareholders into classes, according to the type of claim they have against he firm The court ranks claims in order or priority. Committees representing each class are then formed. The committees negotiate with the debtor firm's management, and with each other if there are divergent interests among the classes.

The firm proposes a reorganization plan,[2] which commonly involves significant changes to the firm's financial structure: existing debt may be reduced or rescheduled, some claims may be exchanges for new securities of the reorganized firm, significant parts of the firm's operations may be sold or closed down, and some claimants (most often common stockholders and junior creditors) may have their claims against or interests in the firm extinguished altogether. The reorganization plan is put to a vote, and, if approved by specified majorities of each class of creditors and by the presiding judge, is said to be confirmed. The company then emerges from bankruptcy. If the parties cannot agree on a plan, the company may be

---

[1] Bankruptcy filings may be voluntary (filed by the debtor) or involuntary (filed by creditors). Involuntary filings usually seek a liquidation of the firm under Chapter 7, rather than a Chapter 11 reorganization.

[2] The firm has the exclusive right to propose a reorganization plan for a certain period (which may be extended by the court), after which creditor committees are allowed to put forward alternative plans.

liquidated, either in Chapter 11 or after conversion to a Chapter 7 "straight bankruptcy" proceeding.[3]

Who Files Chapter 11?

Chapter 11 bankruptcy filings account for a small fraction of all bankruptcy cases, as appears in table 1 below. In 1995, a total of 12,904 Chapter 11 cases were filed, or 1.4% of all bankruptcy filings.[4] Most Chapter 11 cases involve businesses, but even among business bankruptcies, Chapter 11 cases are in the minority. In 1995, the number of business filings (all chapters) was more than 4 times the number of Chapter 11 cases.

Table 1. Bankruptcy Filings for Selected Years, 1980-1995

	1980	1985	1990	1995
Total (Business and Personal Bankruptcies)	331,098	412,431	782,960	926,601
Total Business	43,629	71,242	64,853	52,010
Chapter 11	6,348	23,374	20,783	12,904

Source: Administrative Office of the U.S. Courts

Data showing the size of businesses filing Chapter 11 petitions are not regularly compiled. However, it is generally believed that the larger the business, the more likely Chapter 11 is to be the form of bankruptcy chosen. This does not mean that all or most businesses in Chapter 11 are large corporations. From 1980 through 1994 (the Bankruptcy Reform Act of 1978 took effect in the 4th quarter of 1979), about 275,000 Chapter 11 bankruptcies were filed. By contrast, only 1,213 bankruptcy cases commenced during that period involved publicly owned corporations whose stock was traded on the New York and American stock exchanges or in the over-the-counter market.[5] Most Chapter 11 cases are filed by small

---

[3] For a more detailed discussion of the provisions of Chapter 11, see: U.S. Library of Congress. Congressional Research Service. *A Bankruptcy Primer: Liquidation and Reorganization Under the United States Bankruptcy Code.* CRS Report 94-302 A, by Robin Jeweler. February 17, 1995. 74 p.

[4] These and subsequent figures on the number of bankruptcy filings come from the Administrative Office of the U.S. Courts.

[5] McHugh, Christopher M., ed. *1995 Bankruptcy Yearbook and Almanac.* Boston, New Directions Research, Inc., 1995. p. 226.

businesses and even individuals – 155 of all Chapter 11 cases commenced in 1994 were classified "non-business."

Even with the limited statistical data available, one conclusion stands out. Chapter 11 filings have contributed little to the dramatic increase in total bankruptcy filings observed in the 1980s and 1990s: while the number of total filings has continued to rise,[6] Chapter 11 cases hit a peak in the mid-1980s and have declined since. The bankruptcy "explosion" of the past 15 years has been driven by individual, or personal bankruptcies.

Chapter 11's Predecessors

The concept of reorganization, rather than liquidation, of troubled businesses dates to the mid-19th century. In its earliest form, the process was known as equity receivership. the firm, or a friendly creditor, would petition the court to appoint a receiver to run the business. Reorganization of the firm's finances would then take place by negotiation among creditors and other interested parties. A firm reorganizing in this manner was *not* bankrupt; equity receivership was not a provision of bankruptcy law.[7]

A number of perceived defects in equity receivership led Congress to amend the law in 1934 and again in 1938, bringing business reorganization into the ambit of the bankruptcy code. The most important deficiencies were the following[8]:

- *A cumbersome and precarious legal mechanism.* An ancillary receiver had to be appointed for each jurisdiction in which a company did business. There was no way to control dissenting minorities (creditors who opposed the reorganization effort) except through cash payments. The procedure could be protracted, with no control over legal fees. Finally, the threat of supervening bankruptcy was always present, which could force the firm into liquidation.
- *Domination of the process by large banks and debt underwriters.* These groups often took control of the reorganization, disclosing

---

[6] Data through mid-April suggest that the total number of bankruptcy filings in 1996 may exceed one million.

[7] For a more thorough discussion of equity receivership, see: Dodd, E. Merrick, Jr. Reorganization through Bankruptcy: A Remedy for What? *Harvard Law Review*, v. 48, May 1935. p. 1100-1137.

[8] This discussion follows Dodd, op. cit., and Moore, James W. *Moore's Bankruptcy Manual.* Albany, Matthew Bender & Co., 1939. p. 489-490.

little financial information to other creditors and stakeholders, and taking advantage of "opportunities for self-aggrandizement and oppression" of other interests.[9] It was also suspected that misdeeds of management might be covered up, and that firms that ought to be liquidated would be kept alive.

The legislation enacted in the 1930s sought to remedy these problems by making reorganization part of bankruptcy law. The result, in 1934, was a new Section 77b of the bankruptcy code (P.L. 73-296). This reform did not prove satisfactory for long: it was described as "rather a series of *ad hoc* concessions to the views of different groups than a carefully worked out compromise between them."[10]

In 1938, Congress passed the Chandler Act (which formed the basis of reorganization law until the Bankruptcy Reform Act of 1978), with the twin aims (corresponding to the two major defects in the old procedure) of guarding against fraudulent practices and facilitating honest reorganizations. This was in part a response to the growing complexity of industry and the financial structures of publicly traded corporations:

Local partners have been supplanted by nationwide investors. The consequence is that what was once a simple field of legislative conflict with two readily discernible and widely separated economic forces has come to be a terrain populated by numerous, shifting, and kaleidoscopic contingents. Once the lines were finely drawn; now the boundaries are vague and indistinct; once the forces were wholly economic; now they are shot with social and ethical tinges.[11]

Accordingly, the Chandler Act created a new procedure, Chapter X, which applied only to large firms, and subjected them to a much higher degree of outside scrutiny and control. In Chapter X, existing management of a large firm would always be replaced by a court-appointed trustee. In all Chapter X cases where a firm's total indebtedness exceeded a specified threshold, the reorganization plan had to be submitted to the Securities and Exchange Commission (SEC) for examination and report. Copies of the SEC's report had to be sent to security holders before they voted on a plan of reorganization.

---

[9] Dodd, *Reorganization Through Bankruptcy*, p. 1111.
[10] Ibid.
[11] U.S. Congress. Senate. Special Committee to Investigate Receivership and Bankruptcy Proceedings in the Courts of the United States. *Receivership and Bankruptcy Investigation*. Report No. 2084, 75th Cong., 3rd sess. June 7, 1938. p. 9.

Reorganization of smaller firms was provided for by Chapter XI, under what was called an arrangement procedure. This process involved much less financial disclosure – it was envisioned that firms using Chapter XI would not have stock and bonds in the hands of public investors. In contrast to Chapter S, the firm's existing management remained in control. The scope of reorganization permitted under Chapter XI was limited: unsecured debt could be adjusted, but not secured debt or equity interests.

By the 1970s, a number of problems with reorganization law had emerged, as reflected in the legislative history of the Bankruptcy Reform Act of 1978. The Chapter X process was thought to be too rigid and formalized, too time consuming, and nearly "unworkable" in practice.[12] Many large firms attempted to avail themselves of the simpler Chapter XI procedure; the result was wasteful and expensive preliminary litigation (often initiated by the SEC).

Thus emerged Chapter 11, combining features of Chapters X and XI into a single, one-size-fits-all procedure. Under the new law, the reorganization plan was not bound by strict financial rules, but was to be arrived at by negotiation among the parties after full financial disclosure.[13] What was sought was to fuse the flexibility of Chapter XI with the substantive public protections of Chapter X. Now, in turn, the efficacy of Chapter 11 is debated. Even the briefest history of business reorganization indicates how difficult it has been to craft a wholly satisfactory reorganization procedure; the economic analysis of business failure and the conflicting interests that inevitably come into play suggest why this should be so.

THE ECONOMIC ISSUES

The Economic Premise of Chapter 11

In the legislative history of the Bankruptcy Reform Act of 1978, the rationale behind the adoption of Chapter 11 appears to be essentially economic:

---

[12] U.S. Congress. House. Committee on the Judiciary. *Bankruptcy Reform Act of 1978*. Report, 95th Cong. 1st sess., on H.R. 8200, September 8, 1977. (House Report 95-565) p. 221.
[13] Ibid., p. 223.

The purpose of a business reorganization case, unlike a liquidation case, is to restructure a business's finances so that it may continue to operate, provide its employees with jobs, pay its creditors, and produce a return for its stockholders. The premise of a business reorganization is that assets that are used for production in the industry for which they were designed are more valuable than those same assets sold for scrap. Often, the return on assets that a business can produce is inadequate to compensate those who have invested in the business. Cash flow problems may develop, and require creditors of the business, both trade creditors and long-term lenders, to wait for payment of their claims. If the business can extend or reduce its debts, it often can be returned to a viable state. It is more economically efficient to reorganize than to liquidate, because it preserves jobs and assets.[14]

Since all the economic issues in the debate over Chapter 11 involve this rationale in one way or another, it is worth analyzing in some detail. To economists, business failure is not always undesirable. Economic efficiency – the production of the maximum amount of goods or services from a given amount of inputs – requires that resources be allocated to their most productive uses. Competition, advances in technology, changes in consumer tastes and preferences, and other factors ensure that productive resources must be continually redeployed to find their best uses. This dynamic process of allocation and reallocation entails what has been called creative destruction, "that process of incessant rise and decay of firms and industries which is the central...fact about the capitalist machine."[15]

The formation and dissolution of business enterprises are both key to the achievement of economic efficiency. Firm closing has two dimensions: there is a microeconomic aspect – how is the decision to cease operation reached, and by whom – and a macroeconomic aspect – what is the long-term economic effect of an upsurge in firm closings attributable not to internal factors unique to the individual firms, but to a general state of recession throughout the industry or the economy. Chapter 11, or any other intervention into the firm closing process, has both micro- and macroeconomic implications.

Microeconomic Decisionmaking

When a firm is in financial distress, how does it decide whether to continue operating or shut down? In a market economy, efficiency depends

---

[14] *Bankruptcy Reform Act of 1978.* (House Report 95-595), p. 220.
[15] Schumpeter, Joseph A. *Business Cycles, Volume 1.* New York, McGraw-Hill, 1939. p. 96.

on individual entrepreneurs and investors putting their money at risk where they think the return will be highest. However, once the initial investment has been made, and funds have been committed, the question of whether to operate or close a business changes. One can no longer choose from the full range of available investments, but rather must seek the greatest return possible from the particular assets in which one has invested. Because some of the money spent in establishing a business is not recoverable, the original investment is no longer available to be redeployed, even if the enterprise does not work out as well as one had hoped. Expenditures on advertising, for example, cannot be recouped if the business is closed – these and similar costs are called sunk costs. If a business closes, sunk costs will be lost. Thus, it sometimes makes sense – is economically efficient – to continue operations even when a firm is losing money.

Therefore, while in the long run a money-losing firm must fail, in the short run it can be more costly to close the firm than to keep operating at a loss. In this situation, conflict is likely to emerge among different interests in the firm. Chief among these groups, which tend to act in concert when a firm is operating profitably, are the following:

1. *Equity holders* – the shareholders, or owners of the firm, to whom accrues what remains of the firm's earnings once all other claims against the firm have been met;
2. *Creditors* – bondholders, lenders, and others (such as suppliers who have not yet been paid); and
3. *Workers and managers* (who may also be the equity holders in a privately held business).

In a troubled business, these groups operate under different incentives. Asked whether a firm should be closed, they are likely to provide different answers, as follows:

1. Equity holders receive what is left over after the costs of production and creditors' claims have been paid. In bankruptcy literature, they are called the "residual claimants." They have an incentive to maximize the firm's value, since the increase in value will flow to them.

If, however, the firm's liabilities appear to exceed its assets, equity holders have no interest in preserving the value of the remaining assets, since all the value will be claimed by creditors. Thus, their incentive is to avoid liquidation for as long as possible, on the chance that the business may improve. At the same time, they will have no qualms about investing the firm's remaining assets in extremely risky ventures, since they stand to capture the reward of such investments while creditors bear the risk of further loss.

2. The position of the creditors is nearly the reverse. They are entitled only to the promised return on the funds they have advanced to the firm, and no matter how the firm grows nd prospers, their portion does not increase. Therefore, they have no vital stake in the rehabilitation of a distressed firm, and will be indifferent whether a firm is liquidated or reorganized, *as long as sufficient assets remain to pay them what they are owed*. Their incentive is to maximize the firm's value up to the point at which their claims are covered; beyond that point, someone else will reap the benefits. Since a money-losing firm must sell assets to survive, creditors will frequently favor liquidation over reorganization: they bear the risk of further financial deterioration, while a successful reorganization and the revival of the firm's fortunes will reward equity.

Creditor interests may not be homogenous, especially in large firms. If junior creditors estimate that the firm's assets are sufficient to cover senior debt, but not their own claims, they in effect become residual claimants and have the same incentives as equity holders.

3. Workers and managers want to keep their jobs, regardless of the firm's condition. If a firm is viable as a going concern, they have an incentive to make it work, but if it were better liquidated, they still have an incentive to put off the shutdown as long as possible, even if this means stripping the firm of assets that could have satisfied creditors' claims.

Who is in the best position to decide the fate of the troubled firm? Creditors averse tot he risks of continued operation may press for the prompt liquidation of firms that are good candidates for reorganization. Equity holders, by contrast, have nothing to lose from reckless investment strategies that provide even a slender hope of saving the firm. Employees will generally prefer to continue operation, no matter how unlikely a firm is to survive as a going concern. Chapter 11 provides a framework for negotiation among these parties, from which a plan satisfactory to all may emerge. A good part of the current Chapter 11 debate has to do with whether the negotiation framework favors one party over another. However, the existence of conflicting economic incentives ensures that the process of reaching agreement on a reorganization plan will often be difficult.

Macroeconomic Issues

A recurring theme in the history of American bankruptcy legislation is the need to provide relief for victims of economic hard times. Major legislation tends to coincide with (or follow closely upon) periods of recession. In congressional debates and the associated literature, two conceptions of bankruptcy emerge: involuntary bankruptcy – mechanisms by which the federal courts oversee the debt collection process – and voluntary bankruptcy – whereby debtors gain a temporary reprieve from their debts. The Bankruptcy Act of 1867, which was weighted in favor of involuntary bankruptcy (equity receivership, as noted above, was outside the bankruptcy code) was repealed after the Panic of 1873, and there was no federal bankruptcy law until 1898 (following the severe recession and deflation of 1893-1897). During the consideration of the 1898 law, Representative Oscar W. Underwood of Alabama put the issue thus:

> The only real sentiment in the country is for a voluntary bill to relieve those ruined by financial disasters in the last few years… Where is the man in the south or West who owned a factory, farm, or business house in 1890, that can get today more than 50% of its then value?[16]

Bankruptcy again appeared on the legislative agenda during the Great Depression of the 1930s, when business failure was so common a phenomenon that it was hard to believe that all the failing firms were economically inefficient and were better swept away. The view that wholesale foreclosure and liquidation caused economic damage was expressed as follows, in language prefiguring that of the Senate report (see footnote 14 above) that accompanied the 1978 bankruptcy bill:

> Now, the chief interest of the Nation lies in the continuance of a man's business and the conservation of his property for the benefit of creditors and himself, and not in the sale and distribution of his assets among his

---

[16] Quoted in: Warren, Charles. *Bankruptcy in United States History.* Cambridge, Mass., Harvard Univ. Press, 1935. p. 141.

creditors, or even in his own immediate discharge from his debts. Forced sale of property and stoppage of a business in times of depression constitute loss to the Nation at large.[17]

While contractions in the economy have been relatively mild since the 1930s,[18] concerns that the economy may be damaged by recession-induced failures persist. It has been argued, for example, that if too many firms close during a recession, the economy may face capacity constraints during the ensuing expansion, and one result may be an increase in imports.[19]

Chapter 11 clearly belongs to the "voluntary bankruptcy" tradition; part of its rationale is to provide a countercyclical thrust to limit the harm done by recession. Since it is available to firms in good times as well as bad, however, the microeconomic questions remain. While firms ought to be reorganized and which liquidated? Under what conditions is reorganization likely to be economically beneficial? The assertion that it is more economically efficient to reorganize a firm than to liquidate it depends upon two assumptions:

- The reorganizing firm must be basically sound but experiencing - *short-term* financial distress, resulting perhaps from temporary cash flow problems or from a cyclical business slowdown affecting many firms across an industry or the economy. After reorganization, the firm must be able to produce a return acceptable to the market, otherwise maintaining the firm as a going concern will amount to a long-term subsidy of an inefficient enterprise.

- Liquidation must be destructive of economic value. Under conditions of perfect competition, the invisible hand will direct the reallocation of resources without pain or costs. If there are market imperfections, however (if the market undervalues the firm's assets, if qualified buyers do not emerge, etc.), then the bankrupt firm's assets will not find their best use. As the 1978 Senate report notes, the firm will be sold for scrap, producing losses for all those with stakes in the firm. Another way of stating this assumption is that in order for reorganization to make economic sense, *the value of the firm as a going concern must exceed its liquidation value.*

---

[17] Warren, *Bankruptcy in United States History*, p. 144.

[18] Even so, the 1978 law was deliberated and enacted when memories of the 1973-1975 recession (then the worst since World War II) were fresh.

[19] Hudson, John. The Birth and Death of Firms. *Quarterly Review of Economics and Business*, v. 29, Summer 1989. p. 84.

Whether most Chapter 11 cases meet these tests is debatable. Observers are likely to differ on whether a particular firm ought to be liquidated or whether any given incidence of business failures is excessive. Any reorganization procedure faces two pitfalls. First, it may be too restrictive, with the result that firms that should be reorganized are liquidated. Second, it may be too liberal, allowing firms that should be liquidated to continue to operate. The current debate over Chapter 11 is dominated by those who believe it commits the second of these potential errors.

Bankruptcy and Capital Structure Decisions

In the discussion to this point, firms have been driven to the bankruptcy court by bad luck, bad management, bad economic conditions, or some combination of the three. Another way of looking at the issue, however, is to consider whether the bankruptcy mechanism itself contributes to business failure. An area of economic research bearing on this question is capital structure theory, the study of firms' financing decisions.

Put simply, a firm chooses between debt and equity finance. Is there an ideal mixture or ration that will allow the firm to raise capital at the lowest possible cost? In the traditional approach to the question, it is assumed that a firm with an all-equity capital structure can lower its cost of capital through the use of debt financing, or leverage. (Debt financing is cheaper – other things being equal – because interest payments are deductible from corporate income tax, whereas dividends on common stock must be paid out of after-tax income.) As the proportion of debt in the firm's capital structure (and the risk of default) passes a certain point, however, the firm's total financing costs begin to rise, as creditors demand higher interest rates to compensate for higher risk. Between the two poles of all-equity (forgoing tax savings) and all-debt (with eventual bankruptcy a near certainty), is there an equilibrium point, an optimal debt/equity ratio that will maximize the combined market value of the firm's debt and equity securities, which is the same as saying that the overall cost of capital to the firm will be at the lowest possible level?

The nature of the bankruptcy regime is important in this equation. If the costs of bankruptcy are high, efficiency may suffer in several ways.

[A]n expensive insolvency process will cause firms to sacrifice some of debt's disciplinary benefits. Moreover, whatever the debt level in a firm's capital structure, if insolvency is expensive, fear of insolvency may cause creditors to severely restrict management discretion so that the firm must forego some risky but potentially lucrative projects.[20]

On the other hand, if bankruptcy costs are low, firms may increase their debt burdens to the point where financial fragility becomes an issue. As U.S. firms' debt/equity ratios crept upwards in the 1980s, some economists perceived dangers.[21] Also, critics charged that the Bankruptcy Reform Act of 1978 was too friendly to debtors and was in large measure to blame for the sharp rise in the number of business bankruptcy filings observed in the early 1980s.[22]

The major problem with capital structure theory as an aid to bankruptcy policy is that there is no way to determine an optimum debt/equity ratio. In fact, one of the landmark pieces of modern financial theory – the Miller-Modigliani propositions – holds that the cost of capital to a firm remains constant no matter what debt/equity ratio a firm selects.[23] Nevertheless, a conviction that bankruptcy law affects the incidence of bankruptcy is implicit in many of the recent criticisms of Chapter 11.

CHAPTER 11 IN ACTION

Has Chapter 11 Succeeded?

The most direct and satisfactory way to evaluate the efficacy of Chapter 11 would be to track a representative cross-section of firms that have gone through the process. How many recovered from financial distress and resumed a path of expansion and job creation? How many continued to decline and eventually disappeared? What happened to assets or divisions of firms that were sold during the process? How many jobs were saved?

Unfortunately, these are empirical questions for which there are no empirical data. Schumpeter's 1939 observation remains true today:

---

[20] Adler, Barry E. Financial and Political Theories of American Corporate Bankruptcy. *Stanford Law Review*, v. 45, January 1993. p. 317-318.

[21] Bernanke, Ben. Is There Too Much Corporate Debt? *Federal Reserve Bank of Philadelphia Business Review*, September/October 1989. p. 3-13.

[22] U.S. Library of Congress. Congressional Research Service. *The Bankruptcy Reform Act of 1978 and the United States Economy A Tentative Look at Some Interrelationships.* CRS Report 81-145 E, by Julius W. Allen. June 15, 1981. 26 p.

[23] Modigliani, Franco and Merton H. Miller. The Cost of Capital, Corporation Finance, and the Theory of Investment. *American Economic Review*, v. 48, June 1958. p. 261-297.

Quantitative information about the life span of individual firms and analysis of their careers and their age distributions are among our most urgent desiderata.[24]

The few empirical studies of firms in Chapter 11 focus entirely on the tiny fraction of cases that involves corporations whose securities are publicly traded; for the smaller, privately held firms that account for the vast majority of Chapter 11 filings, financial information is simply not available.

The obstacle to empirical study do not mean that bankruptcy has been ignored in economic and financial research. While the benefits of Chapter 11 are impossible to quantity in our present state of knowledge, there is a large literature that considers the economic implications of legal and administrative arrangements: specifically, what is the nature (and the magnitude) of the costs that arise out of the Chapter 11 procedure?

Direct and Indirect Costs of Chapter 11

Direct Costs

The direct costs of bankruptcy consist of fees paid to professionals – primarily lawyers, but also accountants, investment bankers, appraisers, and so on – and court costs. For Chapter 11 cases involving very large corporations, these fees can add up to many millions of dollars. Direct costs in Chapter 11 cases generally exceed those in Chapter 7, because of the complexity of the procedure, with its negotiating and voting requirements. However, when considered as a fraction of the bankrupt firm's total value, direct bankruptcy costs appear to be relatively modest. Available data, however, are extremely limited. There are only a handful of statistical studies, and most of these deal with cases filed before the current law took effect. The samples are very small (a few dozen firms at most) and not representative of all Chapter 11 cases (that is, studies are limited to large corporations).

The most recent survey covers Chapter 11 cases commenced between 1980 and 1986. For 31 firms listed on the New York or American stock exchanges, direct costs ranged from a high of 6.6^ of the firm's market value at the end of the fiscal year prior to the bankruptcy filing to a low of 1.0%, with a mean cost of 3.1%.[25]

---

[24] Schumpeter, *Business Cycles*, p. 95.
[25] Weiss, Lawrence A. Bankruptcy Resolution: Direct Costs and Violation of Priority of Claims. *Journal of Financial Economics*, v. 27, October 1990. p. 285-314.

Earlier studies found somewhat higher costs, but they involved proceedings under the old, pre-1978 bankruptcy law. Altman surveyed 18 retail and industrial bankruptcies between 1970 and 1978 and reported average direct costs of 4.3% of market value one year before the bankruptcy filing.[26] Warner found mean costs of 4% for 11 railroad bankruptcy cases between 1933 and 1955.[27] Ang, Chua, and McConnell found a higher figure – 7.5% – in their 1982 study of 55 bankruptcies in the western court district of Oklahoma, but they measured costs against the liquidated value of forms at the end of the bankruptcy process. (None of the bankruptcies in their sample concluded with a successful reorganization.)[28]

What is the impact of direct costs on the smaller, privately held firms that make up the great majority of Chapter 11 cases? These costs may be significantly greater than for larger firms when considered as a percentage of total firm value, but reliable data are not available.

The empirical data, even in their present fragmentary state, lead some capital structure theorists to minimize the significance of bankruptcy costs:

> Since the costs of bankruptcy seem relatively small in comparison with the tax advantages of corporate debt, it is difficult to explain the relatively conservative debt policies of many corporations.[29]

The rejoinder is that indirect bankruptcy costs, while harder to measure, may have a greater impact than the fees paid in the course of the judicial proceeding.

Indirect Costs
General Costs of Financial Distress

A firm experiencing financial distress often faces numerous disruptions of its business operations. Suppliers and lenders become reluctant to extend further credit. Sales may decline as customers begin to worry about obtaining service for the firm's products. Employees with skills in demand by the labor market may look for new jobs, and management may be too distracted to make the decisions necessary for the firm to remain

---

[26] Altman, Edward. A Further Empirical Investigation of the Bankruptcy Cost Question. *Journal of Finance*, v. 39, September 1984. p. 1067-1089.

[27] Warner, Jerold B. Bankruptcy Costs: Some Evidence. *Journal of Finance*, v. 32, May 1977. p. 337-347.

[28] Ang, James S., Jess H. Chua, and John J. McConnell. The Administrative Costs of Corporate Bankruptcy: A Note: *Journal of Finance*, v. 37, March 1982. p. 219-226.

[29] Ross, Stephen A. Comment on the Miller-Modigliani Propositions. *Journal of Economic Perspectives*, v. 2, Fall 1988. p. 132.

competitive. These phenomena involve costs to the firm that are significant in capital structure theory in explaining firms' aversion to debt. However, they tell very little about Chapter 11, since they are common to all firms in financial distress. Firms that are liquidated in Chapter 7 and firms that restructure their debts through private agreements (or "workouts") with their creditors incur these costs, as well as firms that reorganize through Chapter 11. However, total distress costs will vary according to the time required for a firm to resolve its financial difficulties one way or the other.

Efficiency Costs of Chapter 11

When a firm enters Chapter 11, the normal structure of corporate governance breaks down entirely. Normally, management runs the company as agents of the shareholders.[30] In Chapter 11, however, this relationship is problematical, since at the end of the reorganization process much of the firm's equity is likely to pass into the hands of bondholders and other creditors.

Creditors are likewise in an anomalous position. Their ability to control management – to protect their own interests – resides largely in their power to force the firm into bankruptcy if interest payments are not made. But, of course, the firm in Chapter 11 is already bankrupt. A deterrent only works until it is used!

In Chapter 11, the interests of stockholders and creditors come into conflict. Stockholders, as noted above, are entitled to what remains of the firm's earnings after costs and expenses, including debt payments, have been met. In bankruptcy, such residual claims are in danger of being extinguished because stockholders generally receive little or nothing until creditors' claims have been paid in full, and the financial position of the bankrupt firm will not often permit this.

Shareholders, then, are likely to favor very high-risk investments, even those with a negative net present value (NPV),[31] where there is a possibility, however slight, of a large payoff. Why shouldn't they? They have little to lose if the investment project fails and if it succeeds they will capture most of the gains. On the other hand, they (or management acting in their interests) might decline to make a different investment with a positive NPV,

---

[30] In small and closely-held firms, management and shareholders are often the same. However, the analysis of shareholder/creditor conflict that follows applies to these firms as well.

[31] the net present value (NPV) is the difference between the present value of future cash receipts from an investment (discounted at the firm's cost of capital) and the initial cash outlay the investment requires. In general, accepting all positive NPV investments maximizes firm value.

if that investment were likely to produce only modest gains that would flow to creditors.

One way to characterize these incentives is to think of equity as a call option on the firm: stockholders' ownership of the firm is unimpaired only after they exercise the option of paying off debtholders. The exercise price of the option is the market value of the firm's debt. In bankruptcy, the option is probably out of the money, that is, the current market price of the firm is below the price at which the option allows it to be purchased.[32] However, the variability, or volatility, of the value of the underlying asset (in this case, the firm) is one component of an option's value. High-risk investment with a chance (however slight) of a high reward has the effect of increasing the variability of the firm's expected future earnings, and thus adds to the value of the stockholders' "option."

The creditor's perspective is different. If the firm's present assets appear to be worth enough to satisfy a creditor's claim, he will naturally oppose high-risk strategies. Creditors bear the risk of loss in this situation without any compensating prospect of gain.

Whose interests should management serve? The law provides only an imperfect guide to fiduciary duties under Chapter 11.[33] In practice, managers tend to put firms in Chapter 11 into a holding pattern:

> Generally, these companies did not start new businesses, make acquisitions not integrally related to the company's existing business, expand significantly the existing business, or engage in other high risk activity. There seemed to be a cultural norm that such investments were inappropriate for a company in reorganization.[34]

Finally, managers and workers have their own incentive to keep their jobs as long as possible, even when this may mean the gradual wasting away of the firm's assets without real hope of renovation.

The essential problem, expressed in terms of efficiency, is that in the normal Chapter 11 situation *no* party's preferred strategy – high-risk, negative NPV investment; a conservative, play-it-safe policy; or a heel-

---

[32] An call option confers the right to purchase an asset at a fixed price. An asset is "in the money" if that price is below the asset's current market price, and "out of the money" (or "underwater") if the exercise price is above the current price.

[33] See: Bienenstock, Martin J. Bankruptcy. *National Law Journal*, v. 16, July 4, 1994. p. B6-B7; and: Roache, John T. The Fiduciary Obligations of a Debtor in Possession. *University of Illinois Law Review*, v. 1993, no. 1, 1993. p. 133-167.

[34] LoPucki, Lynn M. and William C. Whitford. Corporate Governance in the Bankruptcy Reorganization of Large, Publicly-Held Companies. *University of Pennsylvania Law Review*, v. 141, January 1993. p. 748.

dragging forestalling of the inevitable – is likely to maximize firm value, which is necessary if resources are to find their most valuable and productive use. While these efficiency losses arise from conflict among opposed interests within the firm, they ultimately take the form of costs (lost wealth and production) tat are borne by society.

Competitive Effects

Another broad efficiency concern with Chapter 11 is that the automatic stay on debt payments acts as a subsidy to the bankrupt firm as long as it continues to operate its business. A firm that does not have to pay interest on its debt has a competitive advantage, other things being equal, over other firms in the industry or in the local market. If a firm in Chapter 11 seeks to use this advantage to increase market share, the result may be distortions in market pricing with long run harm to the industry as a whole. A recent example was the airline industry, where a few years ago some 20-30% of capacity was accounted for by firms in Chapter 11. There followed price wars that, according to some analysts, weakened the entire airline industry.

Efficiency Costs and the Length of Chapter 11 Cases

While no quantitative estimates of the dollar amount of Chapter 11 efficiency costs are available, it is clear that these costs will rise as long as the skewed investment incentives created by Chapter 11 persist. The time spent in Chapter 11, even for privately held firms, is typically measured in years. Franks and Torous studied 30 cases of firms that emerged from bankruptcy after the confirmation of a reorganization plan: the mean time in Chapter 11 was 3.67 years.[35] LoPucki surveyed a number of published and unpublished studies and reported that while under the previous bankruptcy law the average reorganization case lasted from 5-12 months, under Chapter 11 the mean duration has grown to about 20 months. (Cases involving publicly traded firms last longer – about 24 months, according to LoPucki – but the increase under the new bankruptcy code has not been as marked.)[36]

While some of the length of Chapter 11 proceedings can be attributed to the intricacies of the bargaining and voting mechanisms contained in the law, it is also true that some claimants benefit from drawing out the process as long as possible. Stockholders and others whose interests are underwater (who at that moment stand to receive little or nothing for their claims) have

---

[35] Franks, Julian R. and Walter N. Torous. An Empirical Investigation of U.S. Firms in Reorganization. *Journal of Finance*, v. 44, July 1989. p. 753.
[36] LoPucki, Lynn M. The Trouble with Chapter 11. *Wisconsin Law Review*, v. 1993; no. 3, 1993. p. 740-741.

no interest in a speedy end to the process: there is always the chance that the company's fortunes may take a turn for the better. Returning to the concept of equity as an option to buy the firm, the longer an option has to run, the more likely it is to come into the money. Other things being equal, an option's value falls as the expiration data approaches. The job tenure of managers may be put at risk by the transfer of ownership, so they are not often anxious to conclude the case. Workers facing an uncertain future, of course, prefer to keep their jobs as long as possible. In its complexity, Chapter 11 makes a variety of delaying tactics available.[37]

Managerial Misbehavior

Bradley and Rosenzweig argue that Chapter 11 gives management wide latitude to further their own interests at the expense of others, "to abridge contracts and effectively breach their duties (be they fiduciary or contractual) to security holders while their firms are in reorganization. Chapter 11 allows, indeed encourages, managers to place their interests ahead of the interest of their securities holders and to take actions that they could not take without court protection from creditor scrutiny."[38] They draw these conclusions from the behavior of securities prices and insider transactions involving exchange-listed firms reorganizing both before and after the effective date of the Bankruptcy Reform Act of 1978.[39] According to their analysis of these data, both shareholders and bondholders have suffered considerably greater losses with the onset of bankruptcy under Chapter 11, and the downgrading of bonds of bankrupt firms is more common now than before the 1978 Act. Since both groups, debt and equity holders, have fared worse under Chapter 11 than under the old law, Bradley and Rosenzweig conjecture that corporate managers have been the beneficiaries. They note that corporate insiders sell 25 times more stock in the year before the bankruptcy filing under Chapter 11 than under previous law. In their view, bankruptcy has become less an exogenous event, caused by economic forces and conditions beyond the firm's control, and more of an endogenous one, occurring when it suits management. They liken management's use of Chapter 11 to a defensive tactic in a takeover contest, except that here the defense amounts to an attack on their own firm's security holders. In historical perspective, Bradley and

---

[37] For example, a creditor class can veto a reorganization plan if it can show that it would receive more if the firm were liquidated. Since the value of the firm, either in liquidation or reorganization, is hypothetical (and the figure is arrived at by negotiation) it is difficult and time-consuming to evaluate such claims.

[38] Bradley, Michael and Michael Rosenzweig. The Untenable Case for Chapter 11. *Yale Law Journal*, v. 101, March 1992. p. 1076.

[39] Ibid, p. 1043-1076.

Rosenzweig's attack on corporate management echoes the criticisms of equity receiverships in the 1930s, which led to the adoption of Chapter X, which automatically ousted existing management and required the SEC to scrutinize any proposed reorganization plan.

Other bankruptcy scholars dispute Bradley and Rosenzweig's image of management as the dominant force in Chapter 11, citing the high turnover rates among managers of bankrupt firms. Gilson found that only 43% of CEOs and 46% of directors were still in place at the conclusion of reorganization. (His study included both firms that went through Chapter 11 and firms that restructured privately.)[40] LoPucki and Whitford found that in the 43 cases they studied, 39 firms (91%) had at least one change of CEO during the period beginning 18 months before filing and ending 6 months after confirmation. Thirty-one of these CEO changes came during the Chapter 11 proceeding.[41] In the same study, however, LoPucki and Whitford did observe 8 cases where management was able to negotiate increases in compensation *during* the Chapter 11 process.[42]

Strategic Bankruptcy Filings

There have been several highly publicized cases of corporations filing Chapter 11 not because of long-term financial distress but to avoid the financial effects of a particular event, such as an unfavorable court judgment, a strike, or a previously negotiated labor agreement that the firm now finds onerous.[43] Texaco, A.H. Robins, Continental and Eastern Airlines, Manville, and Dow Corning are among the large corporations that have filed such "strategic" bankruptcies. The threat of a Chapter 11 filing can also be used as a bargaining chip to wring concessions out of creditors or employees.

It also appears that some firms find it comfortable to operate in the Chapter 11 environment.[44] The use of bankruptcy as a business expedient, rather than as a last resort, strikes some as an abuse of the process. In such cases, the law seems to subsidize inefficient businesses or to allow the shifting of costs and risks in ways not intended by Congress.

---

[40] Gilson, Stuart C. Bankruptcy, Boards, Banks, and Blockholders: Evidence on Changes in Corporate Ownership and Control When Firms Default. *Journal of Financial Economics*, v. 27, October 1990. p. 356.

[41] LoPucki and Whitford, *Corporate Governance*. P. 723.

[42] Ibid, p. 740.

[43] For case studies, see: Delaney, Kevin J. *Strategic Bankruptcy*. Berkeley, University of California Press, 1992. 213 p.

[44] E.g., Dickstein, Mark. Macy's Debtor Paradise. *Wall Street Journal*, January 19, 1994. p. A17.

Violations of Absolute Priority

We have seen that delay serves the interest of some parties (typically management and employees or the residual claimants) and works against others (senior creditors). This explains a phenomenon frequently observed in Chapter 11: violation of absolute priority.[45] A basic principle of bankruptcy law is that no claim should be paid until prior (more senior) claims are satisfied; establishing the priority of claims is one of the most important functions of the bankruptcy court. Absolute priority is violated when junior creditors and equity holders share in the distribution of the reorganized firm's securities (or the liquidated firm's assets) before the claims of senior creditors have been fully satisfied. By threatening to delay a settlement through various stalling tactics, junior creditors may be able to extract concessions from senior creditors regarding the terms of the reorganization plan.

Some of the objections to violations of the priority of claims seem to be based on ideas of legal comity rather than economic considerations. Why do deviations from the rule of absolute priority constitute a cost, rather than a transfer from one party to another? If creditors believe they are less likely to be paid back in full, they will demand a risk premium in the form of higher interest rates, raising costs to all borrowing firms. Both Franks and Torous[46] and Bradley and Rosenzweig[47] estimate that the rise in risk premia attributable to the adoption of Chapter 11 may be substantial.

CHAPTER 11 REFORM

The costs of Chapter 11, which was created largely to reduce the costs and rigidities that characterized the previous Chapter X, and, more generally, to avoid the costs of piecemeal liquidation of firms, have led to calls for reform or repeal. We have seen that the costs associated specifically with Chapter 11, rather than all cases of financial distress, arise from problems of corporate governance, conflicts of interest, less than optimal incentives to invest, and the possibility that management may put one group of interests (or its own self-interest) before others. Reform proposals take two approaches to reducing these costs:

---

[45] Occurring in 21 of 27 firms studied by Franks and Torous, *An Empirical Investigation of U.S. Firms in Reorganization*. P. 754.

[46] Ibid, p. 768.

[47] Bradley and Rosenzweig, *The Untenable Case for Chapter 11*. p. 1070.

- Reduce the time firms spend in Chapter 11; and/or
- Replace Chapter 11 with an auction-like mechanism, to quickly determine the highest bidder (and hopefully the highest value user) for a firm's assets. The present reorganization by negotiation under court supervision (a "fictitious sale") would be abolished in favor of a marketplace transaction.

Shortening the Process

The Exclusive Filing Period

One factor that is blamed for the length of Chapter 11 cases is the exclusive right of the debtor firm's management to file a reorganization plan. No one else may propose a plan unless the debtor has not filed a plan within 120 days after the bankruptcy case commences, or unless a plan proposed by the debtor has not been approved by each class of creditors within 180 days. While the debtor has this exclusive right to file, the ability of other parties to move the case forward is limited. Moreover, the bankruptcy judge can extend the period of exclusive right to file, and in many courts approval of requests for extension is routine. It has been proposed to reduce judges' discretion in granting extensions, requiring, for example, that a failure to produce a plan be attributable to circumstances beyond the debtor's control. Section 102 of the Bankruptcy Reform Act of 1994 (P.L. 103-394) took a step in this direction, by providing for a right of immediate appeal to the district court of a bankruptcy court's extension of the debtor's exclusive filing period.

It is worth noting that many Chapter 11 cases are "pre-packaged," which means that the reorganization plan has been informally accepted by creditors before the actual bankruptcy filing. That all firms do not use such procedures is another indication that speeding up the process is not always in all parties' interest.

Small Business "Fast Track" Procedures

The 102nd and 103rd Congresses considered (but did not enact) a proposal to create a new Chapter 10, which would have been an accelerated version of Chapter 11 for small businesses.[48] The filing deadline would have been shortened to 90 days, and a date for the confirmation hearing would be

---

[48] See S. 1985 (102nd Cong.) and S. 540 (103rd Cong.).

set at the time the plan was filed. This idea is a response to the widespread perception that the mechanisms of Chapter 11, perhaps appropriate for large corporations with many types of claimants, are needlessly cumbersome when dealing with the reorganization of most small businesses.

In a sense, the proposed chapter 10 represents a return to pre-1978 law, when there was a Chapter X for public companies and Chapter XI for the rest. Those two procedures, as we have seen, were combined in the Bankruptcy Reform Act of 1978 in part to lower administrative costs and prevent costly preliminary litigation. The proposal to reinstate separate reorganization procedures based on the size of the firm, for essentially the same reason that made consolidation of the two procedures seem desirable twenty years ago, indicates how intractable the problems associated with business reorganization have proved to be.

Section 217 of P.L. 103-394 created a voluntary "fast track" for Chapter 11 cases involving less than $2 million in total debt. If the debtor chooses, the exclusive filing period is reduced to 100 days, creditor committees are eliminated, and certain disclosure requirements are relaxed.

Alternatives to Chapter 11

While an accelerated Chapter 11 might reduce some of the problems of conflict of interest and less-than-optimal incentives, these problems would not be eliminated. Accordingly, more radical reforms have been put forward. These reforms seek to reduce the role of the bankruptcy court, or to remove it entirely from the reorganization process. Under current law, the court essentially does two things. First, it sorts out the claims against the firm and ranks them in order. Then, it conducts a "sale" of the firm (that is, it distributes shares in the new firm in exchange for claims against the old) based on a value that is determined by negotiations among the parties. The conflicts of interest discussed above clearly apply to this process as well: senior creditors will press for a low valuation of the firm, in order that they may receive a bigger share of the new firm, while the residual claimants (be they stockholders, junior creditors, or others) will benefit from a high valuation – if the value of the new firm is judged to exceed what the senior creditors are owed, junior interests will also receive something for their old claims. The valuation process is likely, therefore, to involve prolonged negotiation and to produce a result unsatisfactory to at least some of the parties. A number of proposals seek to avoid this problem altogether by conducting a real (as opposed to judicial or fictitious) sale of the company. The key features of four such proposals are set out below.

Bebchuk[49]

Bebchuk describes his proposal as one that could work within the framework of existing bankruptcy law. Once the court determined the size and relative priority of claims against the bankrupt firm (as it does currently in Chapter 11 cases), all existing claims would be extinguished and replaced with rights in the new reorganized firm. To illustrate, he assumes a firm whose capital structure includes 3 classes of claimants:

- Class A. 100 senior creditors, each owed $1;
- Class B. 100 junior creditors, each also owed $1; and
- Class C. 100 common stockholders, each with 1 share of stock.

At the outset of the reorganization process, each senior creditor would receive one Class A right, entitling him to one share in the reorganized company RC (which is also to have 100 equity shares[50]) *unless* the company redeems the right for $1 (the amount of his claim against the old firm). Each junior creditor receives a Class B right, also redeemable for $1. However, if the company does not redeem the right, Class B creditors receive an option to buy one share of RC for $1. Class C rights are not redeemable by the company, but simply give each old shareholder an option to buy 1 share of RC for $2.

The procedure works as follows: if the Class C stockholders believed that the reorganized firm RC was worth more than $200 (the total debt owned by the old company), they would exercise their rights and become the new owners of RC. The $200 they contributed would be used to redeem the Class A and Class B rights, so that all creditors would have their claims paid in full. (Rights would be fully transferable; if the Class C members could not raise funds themselves, they could sell their options to outsiders. If only some of the Class C rights were exercised, proceeds would be divided on a pro rata basis among the creditors).

If, on the other hand, Class C stockholders decided that RC was worth *less* than $200, they would let their options expire unused, and the choice would pass to Class B. Class B would face the question of whether RC was

---

[49] Bebchuk, Lucian Ayre. A New Approach to Corporate Reorganizations. *Harvard Law Review*, v. 101, February 1988. p. 775-804.

[50] In Bebchuk's procedure, the capital structure of RC need not be all equity, as it is in the illustration. The rights could convert into any combination of debt and equity, so long as the new securities were divided equally among the senior creditors.

worth more than $100. If so, members would purchase the stock of the new company for $100, enough to pay off the claims of senior creditors. If not, control of the entire firm (whose debt burden has been cut in half) will pass to the senior creditors.

An attractive feature of Bebchuk's proposal is that no one can complain of receiving too little value in the distribution of RC shares. If common stockholders (Class C) let their options expire, they get nothing, which is exactly what they would have received had the firm been sold *for their own estimation of its value*. And so on up the ladder of claims: any claimant who thinks the firm is worth more than the value of more senior claims can capture that surplus by exercising his option. The sale/reorganization takes the form of a Dutch auction, where prices are gradually lowered until all merchandise is sold.

The advantages Bebchuk claims for his proposal include a compression of the time frame, which is beneficial both because litigation costs will be smaller and because he believes firms cannot operate efficiently in bankruptcy.[51] In addition, the automatic nature of the procedure takes away the power of junior classes to extort concessions from senior classes, as for example by threatening to draw out the negotiating process. Thus, the absolute priority of claims is more likely to be respected.

Aghion, Hart, and Moore[52]

Aghion, Hart, and Moore adopt Bebchuk's proposal, but graft additional features onto it, giving the bankruptcy court a bigger role. At the same time that rights are allocated, as Bebchuk describes, the bankruptcy court would in addition solicit cash and non-cash bids for the firm (or parts of the firm). The bids will be disclosed *before* the exercise of rights. The new owners of the firm, once they have been determined by Bebchuk's procedure,[53] will then vote on which of the bids, if any, to accept. The process of soliciting bids (which may require evaluation by an investment banker) is designed to provide claimants with better information regarding the market value of the firm before they are called upon to purchase it or let their claims be extinguished. The shareholders' vote provides the opportunity to sell the firm to outsiders (who would also have had the option of acquiring the firm

---

[51] Ibid., p. 780.

[52] Aghion, Philippe, Oliver Hart, and John Moore. *The Economics of Bankruptcy Reform.* Cambridge, MA, National Bureau of Economic Research, 1992. (NBER Working Paper No. 4097) 50 p.

[53] In contrast to Bebchuk, the reorganized firm here will be all-equity.

through the purchase of rights), to retain incumbent managers, or to hire new management.

Aghion, Hart, and Moore consider their proposal an improvement over either Chapter 11 or Chapter 7 procedures. Compared to Chapter 11, they expect their method to reduce litigation costs, to eliminate costly delays (they specify a 4-5 month time frame from beginning to end), and to increase the penalties for management failure. At the same time, they expect to avoid most of the costs associated with liquidations.

Bradley and Rosenzweig[54]

Bradley and Rosenzweig set forth another variation on Bebchuk's reorganization procedure. Their version is more radical, however, in that they would remove the bankruptcy court from the process altogether. The ranking of claims would be determined in advance, as part of debt or equity contracts. Bradley and Rosenzweig propose that a firm in distress sell new equity to enable it to meet its debt payments. Assuming efficient capital markets, this would be possible as long as the value of the firm exceeded the amount of interest owed. If the firm cannot sell equity, the market has determined that there is no net equity position in the firm. Accordingly, when the firm defaults, common shareholders lose all claim to the firm's assets: equity would "evaporate." Simultaneously, the claims of the junior class of creditors would be extinguished, and that class would become the new residual claimants, in effect, the stockholders. They would have two choices: pay off the claims of more senior creditors and become owners of the firm, or have *their* claims extinguished in turn. And so it would continue up the chain of claims, until one class of creditors judged the firm to be worth more than the remaining debt, or until ownership devolved upon the most senior creditor group.

Baird and Jackson[55]

Baird and Jackson are in a sense the forerunners of proposals to radically modify Chapter 11. In separate writings in the mid-1980s, they

---

[54] Bradley, Michael and Michael Rosenzweig. The Untenable Case for Chapter 11. *Yale Law Journal*, v. 101, March 1992. p. 1043-1095.

[55] Baird, Douglas G. The Uneasy Case for Corporate Reorganizations. *Journal of Legal Studies*, v. 14, January 1986. p. 127-147; and: Revisiting Auctions in Chapter 11. *Journal of Law and Economics*, v. 36, April 1993. p. 633-653; and: Jackson, Thomas H. *The Logic and Limits of Bankruptcy Law*. Cambridge, MA, Harvard University Press, 1986. 287 p.; and:

proposed to eliminate Chapter 11 and use Chapter 7 (with modifications to allow the bankrupt firm's operations to continue after filing) as a vehicle to sell the bankrupt firm as a going concern. They recognize that different parties involved in Chapter 11 reorganizations have conflicting interests, resulting in a protracted negotiating process during which the normal incentives for maximizing the value of the firm are absent. The result is economic inefficiency, with social costs as well as the possibility of increasing losses to claimants in the firm. Liquidation is the quickest way to create a new owner who will have the same incentives to manage efficiently as any other business owner. The role of the court, in their view, ought to be primarily to oversee a fair division of the bankrupt firm's assets: this process can, indeed should, be pursued independently of the attempt to find the most efficient use for the assets of the bankrupt firm. They recognize costs associated with auctions, but find that these are probably lower than the costs of reorganization.

Baird and Jackson took up the question again in a pair of 1993 articles, where they seemed less convinced of the advantages of auctions. The chief problem facing a regime of mandatory auctions, in Baird's view, is the uncertain existence of a sufficient number of outside buyers with accurate information about the firm's true condition and value, access to capital, willingness to take risks, and the ability to act decisively once the acquisition is made.[56]

Costs and Benefits of Auctions

The major difficulty with these alternatives to Chapter 11 is their presumption of efficient markets.[57] In an efficient market, investors, such as a class of claimants in the auction models discussed above, would have no trouble raising funds to purchase a firm for what it was really worth. If, in the real world, capital sources are not forthcoming, or if there are market imperfections that result in assets being sold for less than they are worth, at "fire sale" prices in bankruptcy auctions, it is hard to see any advantage in these proposals. The assumption behind Chapter 11, remember is that bankrupt firms are likely to be sold for scrap, with substantial costs to the

---

Comment on Baird, "Revisiting Auctions in Chapter 11." *Journal of Law and Economics*, v. 36, April 1993. p. 655-669.

[56] Baird, *Revisiting Auctions in Chapter 11*. p. 653.

[57] The efficient market hypothesis holds that the market price of a financial asset incorporates all the known information about that asset, and hence reflects its true value.

economy as a whole in terms of economic inefficiency and employment losses.

The evidence regarding the market valuation of bankrupt firms is mixed. If the market systematically undervalues the work of bankrupt firms, an investor ought to be able to earn abnormally high returns by buying the securities of firms in bankruptcy. (Some investors – the so-called "vulture capitalists" – attempt to do just than.) Morse and Shaw investigated this question and found that no abnormal returns were available. They studied firms in bankruptcy before and after the Bankruptcy Reform Act of 1978, and concluded that the new Act had no significant impact on their results.[58]

On the other hand, a later study found evidence of market irrationality in the valuation of bankrupt firm's stock. Schatzberg and Reiber found that stock prices "overadjust" to the news of bankruptcy filings. That is, prices plunge and then recover in a way that is inconsistent with the efficient markets view that prices adjust rapidly and continuously to new information.[59]

The stock exchanges, of course, provide the closest approximation to the perfect markets of economic textbooks. But what of the firms whose securities are not traded on organized markets? They are likely to have much more difficulty in finding buyers, since investors have so little information about them.[60] The key question that must be faced by proponents of bankruptcy auctions is whether qualified buyers will emerge. Shleifer and Vishny put forward an argument that auctions are not likely to produce the buyers that can put the bankrupt firm's assets to the most productive uses. When a firm is in economic distress, other firms in the same industry – whose managers and workers have the expertise to deploy the assets – may also be distressed, and unable to bid. If outsiders buy the firm, they will have to hire managers to run it and will incur agency costs, again depressing bids for firms in bankruptcy.[61]

Others fear that a single buyer would emerge (perhaps the firm's existing management). Without bidding competition, the single buyer could offer a price just above the liquidation value but below the going concern

---

[58] Morse, Dale and Wayne Shaw. Investing in Bankrupt Firms. *Journal of Finance*, v. 43, December 1988. p. 1193-1206.

[59] Schatzberg, John D. and Ronald R. Reiber. Extreme Negative Information and the Market Adjustment Process: The Case of Corporate Bankruptcy. *Quarterly Journal of Business and Economics*, v. 31, Spring 1992. p. 3-21.

[60] Where a firm is not followed by Wall Street analysts and the press, obtaining accurate information (and evaluating it) is costly. These costs will be reflected in lower bids.

[61] Shleifer, Andre and Robert W. Vishny. Liquidation Values and Debt Capacity. *Journal of Finance*, v. 47, September 1992. p. 1343-1366.

value, and pocket the difference. The creditors, if they did not wish to buy and run the firm themselves, would have little choice but to accept. (Of course, under perfect market conditions, the two prices would be identical.)

The chief postulate benefit of auctions is the potential to cut swiftly through the tangle of interests and skewed incentives that characterize large Chapter 11 cases, and to reduce the deadweight costs of lawyers' and other professionals' fees. Investment decisions can be quickly returned to those who have the incentive to maximize the value of the firm. Sale of the firm creates a new class of residual claimants, who must invest wisely because they bear the risk of loss as well as the possibility of gain.

Also present in the proposals to replace Chapter 11 is an uneasiness with the role of management. If the firm goes bankrupt, the reasoning goes, that is evidence of management failure. Why should the same executives who got the firm into trouble be allowed to continue in control? While harsh treatment of managers, as was provided under the old Chapter X, may be pleasing in a certain ethical sense, the economic effects may not be positive. If management knew that a bankruptcy filing would result in a quick sale of the firm (and the loss of their jobs), would they not be likely to run the firm into the ground before filing for bankruptcy? The task of restoring the firm to health, or of finding a buyer, would then be that much more difficult.

Auctions have the potential to relieve some of the problems that seem to be inherent in Chapter 11, but they have costs of their own. Given the lack of empirical data regarding the success of failure of Chapter 11 in its mission of rehabilitation, and the uncertainty regarding the economic assumptions underlying the auction proposals, it is difficult to weigh one set of costs against the other.

CONCLUSION

The Bankruptcy Reform Act of 1994 (P.L. 103-394) created a National Bankruptcy Review Commission, whose mission is to examine the bankruptcy code from top to bottom and make recommendations for reform in a report to Congress due October 20, 1997. While Chapter 11 will certainly be on the Commission's agenda, there is no clear avenue to reform that will ameliorate all the concerns raised about Chapter 11. The costs of Chapter 11 are not one-directional, that is, a feature that one party finds objectionable may work to the benefit of another. For example, some critics of the current system believe that the retention of incumbent management is a drawback – managers may delay the proceedings, may act to enrich themselves, and may not protect the interests of others with claims against the firm. Nevertheless, the presence of managers who have superior information about the firm and its operations may be crucial to Chapter 11's central goal of restoring firms to a viable financial and economic condition.

The process of restoring a distressed firm to health is a costly one, and in many cases may be neither possible nor, from the viewpoint of economic efficiency, even desirable. Is it therefore preferable to put all insolvent firms on the auction block to take their chances with the market? The question would best be approached as an empirical one, but the data to provide an answer are missing. Of the resulting uncertainty, one bankruptcy scholar writes:

> Without that evidence we can only speak in terms of opportunities – opportunities to preserve value, to distribute it according to a deliberate federal scheme, and to reduce the externalization of costs to the public.[62]

Critics have questioned whether Chapter 11 succeeds in fulfilling these opportunities, but have yet to demonstrate that it does not provide them. That may be its best defense.

---

[62] Warren, Elizabeth. Bankruptcy Policymaking in an Imperfect World. *Michigan Law Review*. v. 92, November 1993. p. 376.

INDEX